Reading STREET

Grade **1**

Scott Foresman

Leveled Reader

Teaching Guide

PEARSON

Scott Foresman

Editorial Offices: Glenview, Illinois • Parsippany, New Jersey • New York, New York
Sales Offices: Boston, Massachusetts • Duluth, Georgia • Glenview, Illinois
Coppell, Texas • Sacramento, California • Mesa, Arizona

ISBN: 0-328-16907-2

4 5 6 7 8 9 10 V084 12 11 10 09 08 07 06

Table of Contents

LEVELED READER TITLE	Instruction	Comprehension Practice	Vocabulary Practice
Sam the Duck	12–13	14	15
Look at Bix	16–17	18	19
Rob, Mom, and Socks	20–21	22	23
Time to Eat	24–25	26	27
They Help Animals	28–29	30	31
Animals in the Sun	32–33	34	35
Fun for Families	36–37	38	39
The Play	40–41	42	43
My Neighborhood	44–45	46	47
We Look at Dinosaurs	48–49	50	51
The Forest	52–53	54	55
Worker Bees	56–57	58	59
Nothing Stays the Same	60–61	62	63
Can Hank Sing?	64–65	66	67
A Big Move	68–69	70	71
The Garden	72–73	74	75
Animals Grow and Change	76–77	78	79
Seasons Change	80–81	82	83

Graphic Organizers

Introduction

Scott Foresman *Reading Street* provides over 600 leveled readers that help children become better readers and build a lifelong love of reading. The *Reading Street* leveled readers are engaging texts that help children practice critical reading skills and strategies. They also provide opportunities to build vocabulary, understand concepts, and develop reading fluency.

The leveled readers were developed to be age-appropriate and appealing to children at each grade level. The leveled readers consist of engaging texts in a variety of genres, including fantasy, folk tales, realistic fiction, historical fiction, and narrative and expository nonfiction. To better address real-life reading skills that children will encounter in testing situations and beyond, a higher percentage of nonfiction texts is provided at each grade.

USING THE LEVELED READERS

You can use the leveled readers to meet the diverse needs of your children. Consider using the readers to

- practice critical skills and strategies
- build fluency
- build vocabulary and concepts
- build background for the main selections in the student book
- provide a variety of reading experiences, e.g., shared, group, individual, take-home, readers' theater

GUIDED READING APPROACH

The *Reading Street* leveled readers are leveled according to Guided Reading criteria by experts trained in Guided Reading. The Guided Reading levels increase in difficulty within a grade level and across grade levels. In addition to leveling according to Guided Reading criteria, the instruction provided in the *Leveled Reader Teaching Guide* is compatible with Guided Reading instruction. An instructional routine is provided for each leveled reader. This routine is most effective when working with individual children or small groups.

MANAGING THE CLASSROOM

When using the leveled readers with individuals or small groups, you'll want to keep the other children engaged in meaningful, independent learning tasks. Establishing independent work stations throughout the classroom and child routines for these work stations can help you manage the rest of the class while you work with individuals or small groups. Possible work stations include Listening, Phonics, Vocabulary, Independent Reading, and Cross-Curricular. For classroom management, create a work board that lists the work stations and which children should be at each station. Provide instructions at each station that detail the tasks to be accomplished. Update the board and alert children when they should rotate to a new station. For additional support for managing your classroom, see the *Reading Street Centers Survival Kit.*

USING THE LEVELED READER TEACHING GUIDE

The *Leveled Reader Teaching Guide* provides an instruction plan for each leveled reader based on the same instructional routine.

INTRODUCE THE BOOK The Introduction includes suggestions for creating interest in the text by discussing the title and author, building background, and previewing the book and its features.

READ THE BOOK Before children begin reading the book, have them set purposes for reading and discuss how they can use the reading strategy as they read. Determine how you want children in a particular group to read the text, softly or silently, to a specific point or the entire text. Then use the Comprehension Questions to provide support as needed and to assess comprehension.

REVISIT THE BOOK The Think and Share questions provide opportunities for children to demonstrate their understanding of the text, the target comprehension skill, and vocabulary. The Response Options require children to revisit the text to respond to what they've read and to move beyond the text to explore related content.

SKILL WORK The Skill Work box provides instruction and practice for the target skill and strategy and selection vocabulary. Instruction for an alternate comprehension skill allows teachers to provide additional skill instruction and practice for children.

USING THE GRAPHIC ORGANIZERS

Graphic organizers in blackline-master format can be found on pages 132–152. These can be used as overhead transparencies or as worksheets.

ASSESSING PERFORMANCE

Use the assessment forms that begin on page 6 to make notes about your children's reading skills, use of reading strategies, and general reading behaviors.

MEASURE FLUENT READING (pp. 6–7) Provides directions for measuring a child's fluency, based on words correct per minute (wcpm), and reading accuracy using a running record.

OBSERVATION CHECKLIST (p. 8) Allows you to note the regularity with which children demonstrate their understanding and use of reading skills and strategies.

READING BEHAVIORS CHECKLIST (p. 9) Provides criteria for monitoring certain reading behaviors.

READING STRATEGY ASSESSMENT (p. 10) Provides criteria for evaluating each child's proficiency as a strategic reader.

PROGRESS REPORT (p. 11) Provides a means to track a child's book-reading progress over a period of time by noting the level at which a child reads and his or her accuracy at that level. Reading the chart from left to right gives you a visual model of how quickly a child is making the transition from one level to the next. Share these reports with parents or guardians to help them see how their child's reading is progressing.

Measure Fluent Reading

Taking a Running Record

A running record is an assessment of a child's oral reading accuracy and oral reading fluency. Reading accuracy is based on the number of words read correctly. Reading fluency is based on the reading rate (the number of words correct per minute) and the degree to which a child reads with a "natural flow."

How to Measure Reading Accuracy

1. Choose a grade-level text of about 80 to 120 words that is unfamiliar to the child.
2. Make a copy of the text for yourself. Make a copy for the child or have the child read aloud from a book.
3. Give the child the text and have the child read aloud. (You may wish to record the child's reading for later evaluation.)
4. On your copy of the text, mark any miscues or errors the child makes while reading. See the running record sample on page 7, which shows how to identify and mark miscues.
5. Count the total number of words in the text and the total number of errors made by the child. Note: If a child makes the same error more than once, such as mispronouncing the same word multiple times, count it as one error. Self-corrections do not count as actual errors. Use the following formula to calculate the percentage score, or accuracy rate:

$$\frac{\text{Total Number of Words} - \text{Total Number of Errors}}{\text{Total Number of Words}} \times 100 = \text{percentage score}$$

Interpreting the Results

- A child who reads **95–100%** of the words correctly is reading at an **independent level** and may need more challenging text.
- A child who reads **90–94%** of the words correctly is reading at an **instructional level** and will likely benefit from guided instruction.
- A child who reads **89%** or fewer of the words correctly is reading at a **frustrational level** and may benefit most from targeted instruction with lower-level texts and intervention.

How to Measure Reading Rate (WCPM)

1. Follow Steps 1–3 above.
2. Note the exact times when the child begins and finishes reading.
3. Use the following formula to calculate the number of words correct per minute (WCPM):

$$\frac{\text{Total Number of Words Read Correctly}}{\text{Total Number of Seconds}} \times 60 = \text{words correct per minute}$$

Interpreting the Results

By the end of the year, a first-grader should be reading approximately 45–60 WCPM.

Running Record Sample

Running Record Sample

Beth and her friends were eating ✓ ✓ ✓ ✓ ✓ ✓

(lunch) in the park. ✓ ✓ ✓

"Tell us about your trip to the ✓ ✓ ✓ ✓ ✓ ✓ ✓

beach," Beth said to one of her friends. ✓ ✓ ✓ ✓ ✓ ✓ ✓

"It was great!" her friend said. ✓ ✓ /grēt/ ✓ ✓ ✓ ✓

Beth's friends talked about sports, ✓ ✓ ✓ ✓ ✓ ✓

and they talked about movies. But Beth ✓ ✓ ✓ ✓ ✓ ✓ ✓

was not talking. She was looking away. ✓ ✓ and ✓ ✓ ✓ ✓ ✓

"Beth?" they called to her. ✓ ✓ ✓ ✓ ✓

Beth did not speak. She was looking ✓ ✓ ✓ ✓ ✓ ✓ ✓

at bird. It had landed on a sign. Beth ✓ ✓ ✓ ✓ ✓ ✓ ✓ ✓

just stared. ✓ (sc)

"I have a feeling," Beth said at last. ✓ ✓ ✓ ✓ ✓ ✓ ✓

"What does that mean?" her friends ✓ ✓ ✓ ✓ ✓ ✓

asked. ✓

Beth took out her drawing pad. "I ✓ ✓ ✓ ✓ H ✓ ✓

need to draw that bird, "she said. ✓ ✓ ✓ ✓ ✓ Beth ✓

—From *How Beth Feels*
On-Level Reader 1.4.2

Notations

Accurate Reading
The child reads a word correctly.

Omission
The child omits words or word parts.

Mispronunciation/Misreading
The child pronounces or reads a word incorrectly.

Insertion
The child inserts words or parts of words that are not in the text.

Self-correction
The child reads a word incorrectly but then corrects the error. Do not count self-corrections as actual errors. However, noting self-corrections will help you identify words the child finds difficult.

Hesitation
The child hesitates over a word, and the teacher provides the word. Wait several seconds before telling the child what the word is.

Substitution
The child substitutes words or parts of words for the words in the text.

Running Record Results
Total Number of Words: **103**
Number of Errors: **5**

Reading Time: **136 seconds**

▶ **Reading Accuracy**
$\frac{103 - 5}{103}$ x 100 = 95.146 = 95%

Accuracy Percentage Score: **95%**

▶ **Reading Rate—WCPM**
$\frac{98}{136}$ x 60 = 43.235 = 43 words correct per minute

Reading Rate: **43 WCPM**

Observation Checklist

Child's Name _____ Date _____

Behaviors Observed	Always (Proficient)	Usually (Fluent)	Sometimes (Developing)	Rarely (Novice)
Reading Strategies and Skills				
Uses prior knowledge and preview to understand what book is about				
Makes predictions and checks them while reading				
Uses context clues to figure out meanings of new words				
Uses phonics and syllabication to decode words				
Self-corrects while reading				
Reads at an appropriate reading rate				
Reads with appropriate intonation and stress				
Uses fix-up strategies				
Identifies story elements: character, setting, plot, theme				
Summarizes plot or main ideas accurately				
Uses target comprehension skill to understand the text better				
Responds thoughtfully about the text				

Behaviors Observed	Always (Proficient)	Usually (Fluent)	Sometimes (Developing)	Rarely (Novice)
Reading Behaviors and Attitudes				
Enjoys listening to stories				
Chooses reading as a free-time activity				
Reads with sustained interest and attention				
Participates in discussion about books				

General Comments

Reading Behaviors Checklist

Child's Name _____   Date _____

Behavior	Yes	No	Not Applicable
Recognizes letters of the alphabet			
Recognizes name in print			
Recognizes some environmental print, such as signs and logos			
Knows the difference between letters and words			
Knows the difference between capital and lowercase letters			
Understands function of capitalization and punctuation			
Recognizes that book parts, such as the cover, title page, and table of contents, offer information			
Recognizes that words are represented in writing by specific sequences of letters			
Recognizes words that rhyme			
Distinguishes rhyming and nonrhyming words			
Knows letter-sound correspondences			
Identifies and isolates initial sounds in words			
Identifies and isolates final sounds in words			
Blends sounds to make spoken words			
Segments one-syllable spoken words into individual phonemes			
Reads consonant blends and digraphs			
Reads and understands endings, such as -es, -ed, -ing			
Reads vowels and vowel diphthongs			
Reads and understands possessives			
Reads and understands compound words			
Reads simple sentences			
Reads simple stories			
Understands simple story structure			
Other:			

Reading Strategy Assessment ✓

Child _____   Date _____

Teacher _____

		Proficient	Developing	Emerging	Not showing trait
Building Background Comments:	Previews	☐	☐	☐	☐
	Asks questions	☐	☐	☐	☐
	Predicts	☐	☐	☐	☐
	Activates prior knowledge	☐	☐	☐	☐
	Sets own purposes for reading	☐	☐	☐	☐
	Other:	☐	☐	☐	☐
Comprehension Comments:	Retells/summarizes	☐	☐	☐	☐
	Questions, evaluates ideas	☐	☐	☐	☐
	Relates to self/other texts	☐	☐	☐	☐
	Paraphrases	☐	☐	☐	☐
	Rereads/reads ahead for meaning	☐	☐	☐	☐
	Visualizes	☐	☐	☐	☐
	Uses decoding strategies	☐	☐	☐	☐
	Uses vocabulary strategies	☐	☐	☐	☐
	Understands key ideas of a text	☐	☐	☐	☐
	Other:	☐	☐	☐	☐
Fluency Comments:	Adjusts reading rate	☐	☐	☐	☐
	Reads for accuracy	☐	☐	☐	☐
	Uses expression	☐	☐	☐	☐
	Other:	☐	☐	☐	☐
Connections Comments:	Relates text to self	☐	☐	☐	☐
	Relates text to text	☐	☐	☐	☐
	Relates text to world	☐	☐	☐	☐
	Other:	☐	☐	☐	☐
Self-Assessment Comments:	Is aware of: Strengths	☐	☐	☐	☐
	Needs	☐	☐	☐	☐
	Improvement/achievement	☐	☐	☐	☐
	Sets and implements learning goals	☐	☐	☐	☐
	Maintains logs, records, portfolio	☐	☐	☐	☐
	Works with others	☐	☐	☐	☐
	Shares ideas and materials	☐	☐	☐	☐
	Other:	☐	☐	☐	☐

Progress Report

Child's Name _____

At the top of the chart, record the book title, its grade/unit/week (for example, 1.2.3), and the child's accuracy percentage. See page 6 for measuring fluency, calculating accuracy and reading rates. At the bottom of the chart, record the date you took the running record. In the middle of the chart, make an X in the box across from the level of the child's reading—frustrational level (below 89% accuracy), instructional level (90–94% accuracy), or independent level (95–100% accuracy). Record the reading rate (WCPM) in the next row.

Book Title						
Grade/Unit/Week						
Reading Accuracy Percentage						
LEVEL Frustrational (89% or below)						
Instructional (90–94%)						
Independent (95% or above)						
Reading Rate (WCPM)						
Date						

Sam the Duck

SUMMARY A boy named Jack finds that Sam the duck makes a fine indoor pet.

LESSON VOCABULARY

in   on

way

INTRODUCE THE BOOK

INTRODUCE THE TITLE AND AUTHOR Discuss with children the author and title of *Sam the Duck*. Explain that the author, Alan Levine, wrote the words and that the illustrator, Phyllis Pollema-Cahill, drew the illustrations. Point out the cover illustration that shows a duck in the bathtub and ask children if they have ever seen a real duck indoors.

BUILD BACKGROUND Involve children in a discussion about ducks. Ask them if they know where ducks usually live. Remind them of songs, stories, and poems they know that relate to ducks. If children have seen ducks, ask them to talk about this experience. Ask children if, based on what they know about ducks, they think a duck would make a good indoor pet. Encourage them to give reasons for their answers.

PREVIEW Invite children to take a picture walk through the book. Read the title page and point out the title and names of the author and illustrator. Explain that this information always appears on this page. Tell children that the boy shown on page 4 is named Jack. Ask them to describe the setting of the scene and what the boy is doing. Turn to page 5 and discuss what Jack is doing in this illustration. On page 6, point out the real duck and the rubber ducky in the bathtub. Ask children to predict how the story might end.

READ THE BOOK

SET PURPOSE Help children set a purpose for reading *Sam the Duck*. Model setting a purpose: "From the cover, it looks like this is a story about a duck swimming in a bathtub. That's a really funny idea. I'm going to read more about it." Suggest that children think about the questions and comments that arose as they previewed the illustrations.

STRATEGY SUPPORT: MONITOR AND FIX UP Suggest that children work in pairs or small groups as they read. Encourage them to think aloud and to ask their classmates questions about the text, story, and illustrations. Model questioning: "I wonder if Jack is taking a bath too. What do you think?"

COMPREHENSION QUESTIONS

PAGE 4 Do you think Sam came with his name, or that Jack named his pet? Why do you think so? *(Responses will vary.)*

PAGE 5 Do you think that Sam can understand Jack when he tells him to go on the mat? Why or why not? *(Possible response: No, ducks don't understand people.)*

PAGE 6 Is the bathtub a good place for a duck? Why or why not? *(Possible response: Yes, because ducks like water)*

PAGE 7 What do you think Jack is trying to do? *(Possible response: It looks like Jack is trying to feed Sam something.)*

REVISIT THE BOOK

THINK AND SHARE

1. Responses will vary, but may include that Jack likes Sam or that Jack thinks Sam is a good pet.
2. Jack takes Sam to the tub.
3. *Sam, can, Jack*
4. Responses will vary but may include that Jack has room for a duck.

EXTEND UNDERSTANDING Invite children to discuss the illustrations after they have read the book. Ask: Did the illustrations help you read? Ask volunteers to point out their favorite illustration.

RESPONSE OPTIONS

WRITING Begin a class chart with the predictable sentence pattern *Sam can ___* . Complete the first sentence and then ask each child to suggest a conclusion to the sentence. Write the children's sentences on the chart. Read the chart together. Invite children to copy and illustrate their sentences to make a class book.

MATH CONNECTION

Make a graph to show what kinds of pets children in the class have. List kinds of pets on a chart and have children put a check mark next to the kind of pet they own. Discuss the results: How many pets are there? What kind of pet is there the most of? The least? Does anyone have a duck?

Skill Work

TEACH/REVIEW VOCABULARY

Print the vocabulary words on index cards. Display the cards one a time and read the words as a group. Then ask children to pretend they are writing each word on a large chalkboard. Have them say each letter as they "write" it in the air. After each word is spelled out, have children say the word as they "erase" it.

ELL Give each child a vocabulary word card, and have children find their word somewhere in the classroom. Encourage children to search other books and in environmental print. Invite them to share their discoveries with their classmates.

TARGET SKILL AND STRATEGY

CHARACTER Explain that characters are people in stories. Characters can be real, or they can be made up. In *Sam the Duck*, the main characters are Sam and Jack. Point out to children that when they read, they can think about what characters in a story do and how they feel. Ask: When Jack picked out Sam as a pet, how do you think he felt? How can you tell?

MONITOR AND FIX UP Remind children that what they read should make sense. When they encounter a word they don't know, finding out what the word means can help them understand what they read. They can look the word up in the dictionary.

ADDITIONAL SKILL INSTRUCTION

DRAW CONCLUSIONS Point out to children that as they read, they can use what they have read and what they already know about real life to figure out more about the characters and what happens in the story. Model drawing conclusions. Say: "In the beginning of the story, Jack is with some ducks outside. But then we see Sam. And we see that Sam is with Jack inside Jack's house. You usually don't see animals in a house unless they are pets. Sam must be Jack's pet."

Name_____

Character

1. Show how Jack takes care of Sam. Draw a picture.

2. Would you want Jack to be your friend? (Yes) (No)

_____

_____

Why or why not?

_____

_____

_____

_____

14

Name_____

Vocabulary

Read and trace each word.
Find and circle the matching word.

1.

in   on   of

2.

way   wag   pay

3.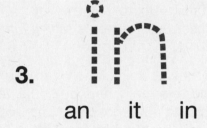

an   it   in

4. Draw a duck *on* the grass.

5. Draw a duck *in* the bathtub.

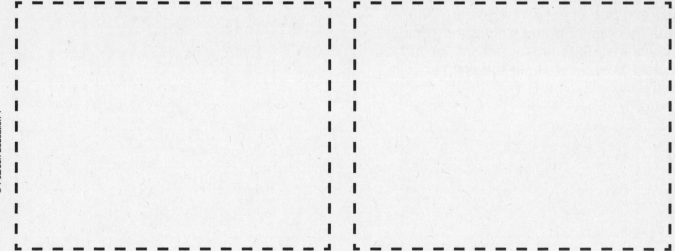

Look at Bix

SUMMARY Bix the yellow Lab gets sick and visits the vet in this realistic story. Colorful photographs accompany the text.

LESSON VOCABULARY

and

take

up

INTRODUCE THE BOOK

INTRODUCE THE TITLE AND AUTHOR Discuss with children the title and the author of *Look at Bix*. Ask: Who is Bix? What is happening to Bix?

BUILD BACKGROUND Discuss what happens when a pet animal gets sick. Ask: Do animals have special doctors? What are they called? Prompt children to recall what they know about veterinarians, based on personal experience, books, and television shows.

ELL Make sure that ELL children understand the role of a veterinarian. Provide a toy stethoscope, bandages, or other medical props and a stuffed animal and have children role-play a visit to the veterinarian.

PREVIEW Have children compare the book's cover and title page. Ask: Are any of the words the same? Is the picture the same? As children look through the book, help them generate questions about the photos. Think aloud: I wonder what is going to happen to the dog?

READ THE BOOK

SET PURPOSE Help children set a purpose for reading *Look at Bix*. Think aloud: I wonder why the dog goes to the doctor. Let's read and find out.

STRATEGY SUPPORT: SUMMARIZE Having children recall a story and retell it in their own words helps them focus on important story events and decide whether the events could really happen or are make-believe.

COMPREHENSION QUESTIONS

PAGE 3 Why is Bix sad? (*Bix is sad because he is sick.*)

PAGE 4 Who is taking Bix to see the vet? (*Possible response: Bix's owner is taking him to the vet.*)

PAGE 5 What is the vet doing? How can she fix Bix up? Could this really happen? (*The vet is examining Bix with a stethoscope. She might give him medicine to make him feel better. This could really happen.*)

PAGE 6 Tell the story in your own words. Tell what happened first, next, and last. (*Responses will vary, but should include beginning, middle, and ending events.*)

REVISIT THE BOOK

THINK AND SHARE

1. Yes, this could really happen. Pets do go to the vet.
2. Bix goes to the doctor; he gets examined; he feels better.
3. *Bix*, *fix*
4. Possible response: I would take my pet to the vet.

EXTEND UNDERSTANDING As children read the book, guide them to pay close attention to details in the photographs. Help them notice the seatbelt on page 4 and the newspaper on page 6.

RESPONSE OPTIONS

WRITING Suggest that children choose their favorite part of the story to illustrate. Have them write a sentence or two to label their illustration.

SCIENCE CONNECTION

Encourage children to find out more about pet care. Suggest that they visit the library to find out what a dog needs to stay healthy and happy.

Skill Work

TEACH/REVIEW VOCABULARY

Print each vocabulary word on an index card. Read the words aloud as a group. Then hold up the word cards, one at a time. Say a sentence containing the word, pausing to allow children to read the word and complete the sentence. For instance: Peanut butter (and) jelly sandwiches are my favorite.

TARGET SKILL AND STRATEGY

REALISM AND FANTASY Point out to children that some stories are make-believe and others could really happen. As children read the book, have them think about whether the story could really happen. Ask: Do the people in the story do things that real people do? Encourage children to give reasons for their responses.

SUMMARIZE Remind children that when they read, they can use their own words to tell what happened in the story. As children read *Look at Bix*, encourage them to think about how they would describe the story to a friend who hasn't read it.

ADDITIONAL SKILL INSTRUCTION

SEQUENCE OF EVENTS Point out to children that understanding what happens first, next, and last in a story helps them remember the story. Demonstrate a three-step process. (For instance, stand up, walk to the board, and write a word.) Ask children to describe what happened first, next, and last. After children have read *Look at Bix*, ask them the first thing, the next thing, and the last thing that happened in the story.

Name _____

Realism and Fantasy

What does Bix do? Draw a picture. Draw one real thing Bix does.
Then draw something a make-believe dog can do.

Real Thing

Make-Believe Thing

Name _____

Vocabulary

Read and trace each word.
Draw a line to connect the matching words.

1. take   and

2. and   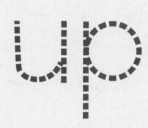

3. up   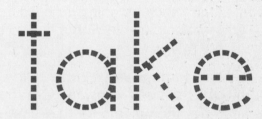

Write each word.

4. take   _____

5. and   _____

6. up   _____

Rob, Mom, and Socks

SUMMARY A boy named Rob and his dog Socks help Rob's mom around the farm in this illustrated story.

LESSON VOCABULARY

get   help
use

INTRODUCE THE BOOK

INTRODUCE THE TITLE AND AUTHOR Discuss with children the title and author of *Rob, Mom, and Socks*. Ask: What does the illustrator do? Ask children to look at the cover illustration and predict where the story might take place.

BUILD BACKGROUND Draw a circle on the board and write the word *farm* in the center. Ask: Do you know what a farm is? Write children's ideas in the circle. Draw another circle and write the word *buildings* inside. Ask children to name buildings they might find on a farm. List these ideas in the *buildings* circle. Expand the farm concept map by drawing circles with additional labels, such as animals, buildings, or jobs. Connect each circle with a line to the "farm" circle.

PREVIEW/TAKE A PICTURE WALK Invite children to look through the book with you. Turn to page 3 and have them compare this illustration to the cover. Ask: Is this the same picture? As children preview the remaining pages, focus their attention on what the boy is doing in each picture. Model interesting vocabulary as you describe the boy's actions. For example, turn to page 4 and say: "The boy is feeding the hogs. What the hogs are eating is called *slop*. Slopping the hogs is another way of saying feeding the hogs." Continue with the rest of the illustrations.

READ THE BOOK

SET PURPOSE Guide children to set a purpose for reading *Rob, Mom, and Socks*. Suggest that they compare the farm in the story to what they already know about farms. What things are the same? What things are different?

STRATEGY SUPPORT: VISUALIZE As children read about Rob, Mom, and Socks's trip to town, prompt them to imagine what the characters experience along the way. Lead children in a guided visualization. Have them close their eyes and picture a car driving down the road. Ask: Is the road smooth or bumpy? What is the weather like? Are there a lot of cars on the road?

COMPREHENSION QUESTIONS

PAGE 3 Why do you think the dog is named Socks? (*The markings on the dog's legs look like socks.*)

PAGES 5–6 How did Socks get so muddy? Why does Rob wash the dog but not the hogs? (*Socks got muddy when Rob was feeding the hogs. Possible response: Rob washes Socks because Socks would get the car dirty.*)

PAGES 3–6 Name the jobs Rob does on the farm. Do you think a boy could really do these jobs? Why or why not? (*Rob helps to wipe the tractor, feed the hogs, wash the dog, and fix the wall. Responses will vary but should relate to children's experience.*)

PAGES 3–6 Does Rob like working on the farm? Why do you think so? (*Rob seems to like working on the farm; he is always smiling.*)

PAGE 8 What do you think Rob, Mom, and Socks will do when they get to town? (*Responses will vary.*)

REVISIT THE BOOK

THINK AND SHARE

1. Drawings may vary but should show a farm setting.
2. They might drive to the store to buy food.
3. *Socks, rags, pails, rocks*
4. Possible response: Rob and Socks could feed the other animals.

EXTEND UNDERSTANDING Ask children to consider whether the story could take place in a different setting. Ask: If Rob and Socks lived in a city, what jobs would they do? What would be the same? What would be different?

RESPONSE OPTIONS

WRITING Suggest that children retell the story from Rob's perspective. Ask them to imagine what Rob might think and say about his daily activities. Have children write and illustrate a few sentences, using pronouns as appropriate.

SOCIAL STUDIES CONNECTION

Time For SOCIAL STUDIES

Encourage children to learn more about tractors and other farm equipment. Gather resources from the library, the Internet, or your local farm bureau. Children can make a class book that describes farm machines.

Skill Work

TEACH/REVIEW VOCABULARY

Write the word *help* on the board. Have children read it aloud and talk about what it means. Then turn to page 6. Read the text together, pausing before *help*. Ask a volunteer to highlight the word on the page with highlighting tape. Repeat for *use* (pages 3–7) and *get* (page 6).

ELL Write each vocabulary word on a word card. Invite English language learners to go on a word hunt. Provide each child with a word card and a sticky note and have children search the classroom for their chosen word. When they find the word, have them mark it with a sticky note. Switch cards and play again.

TARGET SKILL AND STRATEGY

CHARACTER AND SETTING Point out to children that stories have people or animals in them *(characters)* and occur in a certain place or time *(setting)*. Thinking about who is in a story and where it takes place helps readers understand what they read. Discuss Rob's attitudes and behaviors with the children. Ask: When Rob helps Mom with the hogs, what does this tell you about him? Would you like Rob to be your friend? Also discuss the setting of the story. Ask: Where does this story happen? Have you ever seen a place like this?

VISUALIZE Remind children that picturing the story in their minds as they read can help them remember the story's characters and setting.

ADDITIONAL SKILL INSTRUCTION

PLOT Point out to children that every story has three parts: beginning, middle, and end. Work with children to identify the beginning, middle, and end of *Rob, Mom, and Socks*. Record these events on a simple story map.

Name_____

Character and Setting

Rob and Socks help Mom with the hogs.
Rob and Socks use rocks to fix the wall.
Rob and Socks go to town with Mom.

Draw two things that Rob does to help Mom.
Show where the story takes place. Show how Rob feels.

Name_____

Vocabulary

Circle the correct word to finish each sentence. Write the word on the line.

1. Rob and Socks _____ Mom on the farm.

   help   hall

2. Socks will _____ a bath.

   got   get

3. Rob will _____ a hose to wash Socks.

   us   use

Circle the words that sound like **get**.

4. eat   wet   tap

5. sat   feet   set

Time to Eat

SUMMARY In this realistic story, a boy and his mother feed the animals in the barnyard before sitting down to share an evening meal. The story is written in predictable language, with strong illustration support.

LESSON VOCABULARY
eat	her
this	too

INTRODUCE THE BOOK

INTRODUCE THE TITLE AND AUTHOR Discuss with children the title and the author of *Time to Eat*. Talk about the roles of the author and the illustrator. Look at the cover together and ask children to describe what the animals are doing in the illustration. Based on the title and the cover illustration, ask children what they think this story might be about. Who is eating dinner in the picture? Who else might eat dinner in the story?

BUILD BACKGROUND Sing "Old McDonald Had a Farm" with the children. Then involve the group in a discussion about farm life. Remind children of other stories they have read or heard about life on a farm. Talk about the kinds of animals that live on a farm and the role of the farmer in caring for them. Together, brainstorm a list of jobs to be done on a farm. Then ask children to think about how kids might help with this work. Ask: What kinds of jobs could a boy or girl your age do on a farm?

ELL Make sure that English language learners know the names of the farm animals pictured in this story. Use pictures of farm animals to play a matching game in which you call out the sound the animal makes and the children point to the picture and name the animal.

PREVIEW Invite children to look through the book and scan the illustrations. Encourage them to predict what might happen in this story, based on what they see. Point out the boy and his mother on page 3 and discuss the setting of the story and the characters' clothing. Ask children to identify the foods that the animals are eating on pages 4 and 5. Turn to page 7 and ask children to predict how the book might end. Introduce the word *picnic*. If children have experiences eating outdoors, encourage them to talk about this.

READ THE BOOK

SET PURPOSE Help children set a purpose for reading *Time to Eat*. Ask children to review the questions they asked while previewing the illustrations. Suggest that children choose a question from the list and look for the answer as they read. Model setting a purpose for reading: "It looks like the boy is helping his mother. I want to read and find out exactly what they are doing."

STRATEGY SUPPORT: ASK QUESTIONS Point out to children that not every question they generate will be answered in the text. Help them brainstorm ways of finding answers to their unanswered questions.

COMPREHENSION QUESTIONS

PAGE 3 What is this page mostly about? (*The page is about what horses eat.*)

PAGE 4 What are these little animals? What are they eating? (*The little animals are chickens; they are eating grain.*)

PAGE 6 How do the boy and his mother know that it's time for dinner? (*They know it is time for dinner because the mother checked her watch.*)

PAGE 7 Ask one question about this page. (*Responses will vary, but should relate to the text or illustrations.*)

REVISIT THE BOOK

THINK AND SHARE

1. Possible response: The story is about dinner. People and animals all eat.
2. Possible response: What do cows eat?
3. *eats, looking*
4. Possible response: Animals sleep at night.

EXTEND UNDERSTANDING Direct children's attention to the illustrations. Challenge them to find the animal that eats people's leftovers. Ask: What do you think the pig might eat for dinner the next day? Why do you think so?

RESPONSE OPTIONS

WRITING Invite children to write and illustrate a story about animals eating dinner in a different setting. They might write about animals in the forest, the jungle, or the zoo. Encourage them to use a predictable sentence pattern, as modeled in *Time to Eat*.

DRAMA CONNECTION

Invite children to make stick puppets of the various farm animals featured in *Time to Eat* and use them to dramatize the story. Together, make up dialogue for each of the characters in the story.

Skill Work

TEACH/REVIEW VOCABULARY

Write the word *eat* on the board. Read the word together and use it in a sentence. Turn to page 5 and ask children if they can find the word that contains *eat*. Read *eats* together. Repeat for the other vocabulary words.

TARGET SKILL AND STRATEGY

👁 **MAIN IDEA** Turn to pages 4 and 5. Read the sentences together. Then ask: What are these sentences about? Help children understand that both pages are about eating dinner, and that this is the *main idea*. Repeat for other pages.

👁 **ASK QUESTIONS** Remind children that *asking questions* can help them understand and remember what they read. As children preview the selection, model making "I wonder" statements. Turn to page 6 and say: I wonder why the mom is looking at her watch. On chart paper, write: *Why is the mom looking at her watch?* Encourage children to generate their own "I wonder" statements based on the illustrations. List their questions on chart paper, leaving room for responses below. After reading the book, review the questions. Write the answers on the chart, using contrasting ink.

ADDITIONAL SKILL INSTRUCTION

COMPARE AND CONTRAST Point out to children that they can think about how two things are *alike* and how they are *different*. Turn to pages 4 and 5. Read the text and model how to compare the horses to the chickens, using a Venn diagram. Compare characteristics such as where the animals live, how many feet they have, and what they eat. Repeat with pages 6 and 7, asking children to compare the pig and the people.

Name _____

Main Idea

Read the sentences.

> The cat eats this dinner.
>
> The pig is eating her dinner.
>
> The little dog is eating dinner.
>
> Mom and I eat dinner too.

1. What are these sentences all about?

   a) the pig

   b) animals on the farm

   c) eating dinner

2. Draw a picture that shows the main idea.

Name _____

Vocabulary

Read and write each word. Find and circle the matching word.

┌─────────────────────────────────────┐
│ **Words to Know** │
├─────────────────────────────────────┤
│ eat   her   this   too │
└─────────────────────────────────────┘

1. eat _____ cat, eat, fat

2. her _____ her, hem, hen

3. this _____ that, thin, this

4. too _____ to, too, boo

They Help Animals

SUMMARY This fiction reader describes children taking animals to the vet. We also learn that the vet can help our pets.

LESSON VOCABULARY

saw	small
tree	your

INTRODUCE THE BOOK

INTRODUCE THE TITLE AND AUTHOR Discuss with children the title and the author of *They Help Animals.* Encourage children to share what they think this book will be about, based on the title. Ask: Who do you think "they" might be? What animals do you think they help?

BUILD BACKGROUND Invite children to share what they know about animals. Have them describe animals they have seen, at home or elsewhere. Encourage children to share what they know about these animals, including what they look like, what sounds they make, and how to care for them.

PREVIEW Have children preview the book by flipping through the pages and looking at the illustrations. Encourage children to describe what they see happening on each page. Ask: What animal(s) do you see here? What is this person doing with the animal(s)? Where are they?

READ THE BOOK

SET PURPOSE Based on your preview of the book, guide children in setting a purpose for reading. Ask them what they would like to learn or find out about the story. After looking at the illustrations, have children predict what animals they think they will learn about in the story. Encourage children to share their favorite illustrations and why they would like to know more about these animals, people, or what they are doing.

STRATEGY SUPPORT: STORY STRUCTURE Help children better understand the structure of the story by writing a simple outline or graphic organizer on the board. Use the words *beginning, middle,* and *end* to sequence the information. Also use signal words such as first, next, then, and last as you discuss the story and elicit information from children.

COMPREHENSION QUESTIONS

PAGE 3 What happened first in the story? *(He saw a sick bird.)*

PAGE 4 Then what did the boy do next? *(He took the bird to the vet.)*

PAGES 5–6 The story tells us that a boy saw a small cat and took it to the vet. Could this really happen, or is it make-believe? *(It could really happen.)*

PAGE 7 What did we learn from this story? *(Vets can help animals.)*

REVIST THE BOOK

THINK AND SHARE

1. Responses will vary but might include dogs, gerbils, horses, etc.
2. Plot: A boy finds a bird and brings it to the vet; the vet helps the animals.
3. *grass*
4. Responses will vary but might include a parent, another relative, or a teacher.

EXTEND UNDERSTANDING Call children's attention to the *Animal Shelter* sign in the illustrations on pages 4 and 6. Help children read these words and discuss how this sign helps us better understand the story. Ask: Would it be as easy to understand where the characters were taking the animals if the *Animal Shelter* sign were not there? Encourage children to tell about the different signs and environmental print they see around them every day and how this information helps us.

RESPONSE OPTIONS

SPEAKING Write the following sentences from the story on the board. *I saw a _____. Take the _____ to the vet.* Have children think of ways to complete the idea and then take turns saying the first sentence aloud to the class. The rest of the group then repeats the second sentence to complete the exchange. You may wish to model how to do this to get children started. Say: I saw a sick hamster. Then have the children say: Take the hamster to the vet. If children are able, extend this exercise by having them copy and complete the sentences on their own papers.

SCIENCE CONNECTION

Explore different ways we can help animals. Discuss with children why we take animals to the vet and what shelters or other rescue organizations can do for animals. If possible, invite a veterinarian or animal rescue worker to come speak to the class. The children may even wish to participate in an activity to help animals, such as fundraising or collecting items such as food and bedding to donate to a local animal shelter.

Skill Work

TEACH/REVIEW VOCABULARY

Have children write down each of the vocabulary words on their own papers saying the words as they do so. Help children think of sentences using each word and repeat these to each other.

ELL Encourage English language learners to say the vocabulary words in their home languages and write the words on their papers. Give them sentences using each word and ask them to repeat the sentences.

TARGET SKILL AND STRATEGY

REALISM AND FANTASY Explain to children that some stories could really happen and others are make-believe, (or fantasy) meaning they could not really happen. After reading *They Help Animals,* ask children to determine whether this story could really happen or if it is make-believe. Ask: What happens in this story that makes you think it really could happen?

STORY STRUCTURE As children read, remind them that all stories have a beginning, middle, and end. This is called *story structure.* Ask: What happens at the beginning of the story? (*A boy saw a hurt bird and took it to the vet.*) the middle? (*Another boy saw a small cat and took it to the vet.*) the end? (*The vet can help many animals.*)

ADDITIONAL SKILL INSTRUCTION

THEME Explain to the children that every story has a "big idea" or theme. This "big idea" is what the story is all about, and might even be a lesson that we learn from the story. Guide children in determining the big idea in *They Help Animals.* Model for them how to determine the big idea. Ask: What did we learn from reading this book? What is this story all about?

Name _____

Realism and Fantasy

Some stories, like *They Help Animals*, could really happen. Other stories are make-believe. Some of the things in the list below are from the story. Circle the things that tell you *They Help Animals* could really happen. Then think about why the items you did not circle are make-believe.

1. a hurt bird

2. a talking dog

3. a bird that says "moo"

4. a small cat

5. the vet helps animals

6. Think about one thing that you did not circle. Write a sentence to explain why.

_____

- -

_____

Name _____

Vocabulary

Choose the word from the box that best completes each sentence.

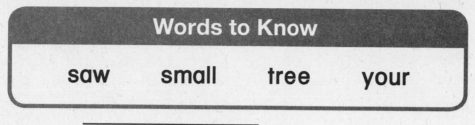

Words to Know

| saw | small | tree | your |

1. The cat was _____ .

2. I _____ a dog.

3. The vet can help _____ pets.

4. The bird was in the _____ .

5. The word *saw* has more than one meaning. Draw a picture that shows another meaning of *saw*.

Animals in the Sun

SUMMARY Children learn about how animals cool down in the hot sun. Photographs of animals playing in the water capture children's imagination and activate their experiences of playing in water.

LESSON VOCABULARY

home	into
many	them

INTRODUCE THE BOOK

INTRODUCE THE TITLE AND AUTHOR Discuss the title and the author of *Animals in the Sun*. Ask children to look at the photograph on the cover and comment on how it relates to the title. Ask children in what kind of area the book might take place.

BUILD BACKGROUND Encourage discussion about what children do on a hot summer day. Ask: Do you like to drink cold lemonade? Do you like to play with a hose or swim? How does water make you feel?

PREVIEW Have children look at each picture in the book. Encourage them to name the animals they can. Ask if any children have seen any of the animals in other contexts, such as at a zoo or in another book.

READ THE BOOK

SET PURPOSE Model how to set a purpose for reading by commenting on the photograph on the cover. Say: "The sun looks very hot! I want to read this book to see what animals do when it is very hot." Prompt students to tell their own purposes for reading the book.

STRATEGY SUPPORT: MONITOR AND FIX UP As children learn to *monitor* and *fix up* their understanding of text, they need to be aware of whether the text makes sense. Self-questioning can help them check their understanding. Model self-questioning by pausing after reading page 3. Say: "I am not sure if I understand how animals can *build* homes in this place. Maybe *make their homes* just means that the animals *live* here." Encourage children to stop and ask questions when they do not understand the text.

COMPREHENSION QUESTIONS

PAGE 4 Why is it hot? (*because the sun is shining*)

PAGE 5 What are the hippos doing in the photograph? (*They are cooling off in the pond.*)

PAGE 6 Where are the elephants going? (*They are going to the pond.*)

PAGE 7 Is the pond very deep? How do you know? (*no, because it only comes up to the tops of the zebras' legs*)

PAGE 8 Which animals use the pond to cool off? (*hippos, elephants, and zebras*)

REVISIT THE BOOK

THINK AND SHARE

1. Possible response: They went into a pond to cool off.

2. hippos, elephants, and zebras

3. *fun, sun*

4. Page 8 shows three different kinds of animals.

EXTEND UNDERSTANDING Have children look at the photograph of the hippos on page 5. Ask: What can you learn about hippos from this photograph? *(Possible responses: They can open their mouths wide; they have tiny ears.)* Continue in a similar fashion with the other photographs.

RESPONSE OPTIONS

SPEAKING Have children describe to others what they do to stay cool.

ELL Write the words *elephant*, *hippo*, and *zebra* on a piece of paper, allowing room between each word. Make copies of the paper for each ELL and ask them to draw a picture of the animal underneath its name.

SCIENCE CONNECTION

Assist children in doing research on the African savannah and animals mentioned in *Animals in the Sun,* using books, children's wildlife magazines, and the Internet. Have each child choose one aspect of this environment and write a sentence about it. Then have children use large construction paper to make cutouts representing the characteristics or animals they have chosen. Attach their sentences to the backs of their cutouts. Create a savannah tableau with children standing, holding their cutouts, reading their sentences in turn. Invite another class to observe. Allow the children to answer questions about the parts of the savannah they represent.

Skill Work

TEACH/REVIEW VOCABULARY

Have children take turns using each vocabulary word in a sentence. Have them say their sentences aloud to the group as you write their sentences on the board.

ELL Many children, especially English language learners, think of *home* and *house* as completely interchangeable. Explain the meaning of *house* as the building in which people or certain animals live, while the broader meaning of *home* includes houses, places, countries, and habitats.

TARGET SKILL AND STRATEGY

CAUSE AND EFFECT Draw attention to *cause-and-effect* relationships by asking children to think as they read about what is happening and why those things are happening. Say: Look at pages 5, 6, and 7. What happened? Why did it happen?

MONITOR AND FIX UP Looking at the photographs can help children *monitor* and *fix up* their comprehension of the text. It will also help children make the connections between the cause-and-effect relationships in this book. A good example is found on page 8. Ask children to look at the pictures and discuss why the animals went to the pond.

ADDITIONAL SKILL INSTRUCTION

AUTHOR'S PURPOSE Begin prompting children to identify the *author's purpose* by identifying the author. Before children read the book, ask: Who wrote this book? What do you think the book will be about? Why? How do you think you will feel or think about animals and the sun after reading this book? Why? Do you think this book is funny, sad, serious, or exciting? Lead children to explain their answers by identifying features or facts in the text. Record children's answers to discuss after reading. Allow for multiple correct responses to emphasize that authors can have more than one purpose.

Name _____

Cause and Effect

Directions Think about what happened in the story. Then think about why it happened. Write a word from the story that best fits into each sentence.

_____

1. The sun is _____ .

_____

2. Animals have _____ in the sun.

_____

3. The animals are hot. So they run into a _____ .

4. Draw a picture of something you like to do when you are hot.

34

Name _____

Vocabulary

Draw a picture of the meaning of the word in each box.

1. home	2. into
3. many	4. them

Fun For Families

SUMMARY This nonfiction book asks what families can do and then describes some of the different things families can do together through both photographs and text.

LESSON VOCABULARY

catch	good
no	put
want	

INTRODUCE THE BOOK

INTRODUCE THE TITLE AND AUTHOR Discuss with children the title and the author of *Fun For Families.* Invite them to look at and describe what they see happening in the photographs on the cover. Ask: What do you think these people have in common? What are they doing together? Do they look like they are having fun? What makes you think so? Based on the title and their discussion of the photographs, invite children to predict what the book will be about.

BUILD BACKGROUND Engage children in a discussion about their families. Ask: What are some things that you do with your family? What is your favorite thing to do with your family? Why do you enjoy doing these things with your family? Do you think it is important to spend time with your family? Why?

PREVIEW/TAKE A PICTURE WALK Invite children to preview the book, looking at the photographs. Ask them to describe what they see happening on each page and make predictions about the text. Ask: Where do you think this family is? What are these people doing?

READ THE BOOK

SET PURPOSE Guide the children in setting a purpose for reading. Discuss the title of the book, *Fun For Families.* If children need help setting a purpose, model for them: "I am curious to know more about these people on the cover and what they are doing, so I am going to read to find out."

STRATEGY SUPPORT: PREDICT Encourage children to use their own knowledge and experience in making predictions. Help them think about why and how they make predictions. Ask children to predict what might happen next with the family on page 4 and have them describe why they think about this. You might use these questions: What made you think they would cook the fish for dinner? How do you think the fish will taste? How do you know about how a fish tastes?

COMPREHENSION QUESTIONS

PAGES 4–5 What are the families on these pages doing? *(catching fish for dinner, playing ball)*

PAGE 7 What do you think this family will do next? *(Responses may vary: go home, make dinner)*

PAGE 8 This page says that families want to have fun together. What fun things do you see the families doing in these photographs? *(doing artwork outdoors, swinging)*

REVISIT THE BOOK

THINK AND SHARE

1. Families enjoy doing different things together.
2. Pictures will vary but might include the family cooking or eating.
3. *fish, with*
4. two

EXTEND UNDERSTANDING After reading, have children look again at the photographs in the book. Call their attention to the single images at the bottom of pages 4–7 and encourage them to describe how each item relates to the main picture and the text. Ask: What is this? What does it have to do with the main picture? How does it help us understand the main picture? How do the two pictures together help us understand the words on the page?

RESPONSE OPTIONS

WRITING Help each child write a few words or a sentence on a piece of paper explaining his or her favorite family activity. Then children can draw and illustrate these activities. Encourage children to share their pictures and read their sentences to the class. Have them explain why they enjoy doing these activities with their families.

SOCIAL STUDIES CONNECTION

Time For
SOCIAL
STUDIES

Provide children with magazines and ask them to cut out pictures of families doing things together. Gather all of the pictures together and create a collage titled "Fun For Families." Assist children in writing labels for the pictures, such as camping, shopping, eating dinner. Children may also enjoy bringing in photographs of their own families to add to the collage.

Skill Work

TEACH/REVIEW VOCABULARY

Have children write each of the vocabulary words on their own papers, saying the words as they do so. Help children to think of sentences using each word and repeat these to each other.

ELL Encourage English language learners to write and say the vocabulary words and think of how to say the words in their home languages. Give them a sentence using one of the words to read and repeat with you.

TARGET SKILL AND STRATEGY

MAIN IDEA Draw children's attention to page 4. Read the sentence aloud together, and then ask: What is this sentence all about? Encourage children to describe the main idea in just a few words. If children have difficulty naming the main idea on their own, give several options from which they can choose. Ask: Is the main idea that families can catch fish, eat fish, or cook fish?

PREDICT After reading page 4, encourage children to predict what might happen next. Ask: After this family catches a fish, what do you think they will do next? What do you think they will do if they don't catch a fish?

ADDITIONAL SKILL INSTRUCTION

DRAW CONCLUSIONS Turn to page 6 and discuss the picture. Ask: What is this family doing? Look at their faces. How do you think they feel? Does it look like they are having fun? What makes you think that?

Name_____

Main Idea

Think about what you read in *Fun For Families*.
Circle the letter of the answers to the questions.

_____

1. What is the book about?

    a. playing ball

    b. families

    c. small kids

> They can play catch with a ball.

2. What is the sentence in the box all about?

    a. Families go to bed.

    b. Families play ball.

    c. Families eat dinner.

3. Draw a picture of something your family can do.

38

Name_____

Vocabulary

First read the three names for things.
Then pick a word from the word box that completes the idea.

| Words to Know |
| catch   good   no   put   want |

---

1. Clothes

Books

Toys

Things that you _____ away

---

2. Fish

Ball

Butterfly

Things that you _____

---

3. Ice cream

Lemonade

Popsicle

Things that you _____ on a hot day

---

4. Apple

Carrots

Celery

Things that are _____ for you

The Play

SUMMARY In *The Play*, a class works together to stage a dramatic performance for their parents. The simple, repetitive text describes each step of the preparation process.

LESSON VOCABULARY

be	could	horse
old	paper	

INTRODUCE THE BOOK

INTRODUCE THE TITLE AND AUTHOR Discuss with children the title and author of *The Play*. Ask children what kinds of things they might expect to read about in a book called *The Play*. Examine the cover illustration together and encourage children to describe the various costumes the characters in the book are wearing. Turn to the title page and compare the illustration on this page to the cover illustration. Ask children to read the title and names of the author and illustrator. Point out that the title page always contains this information.

BUILD BACKGROUND Invite children to discuss their personal experience with plays. If children have performed in a play, ask them to talk about what they did to prepare for the show. If children have attended a play, discuss the roles of the performers and the audience.

PREVIEW Lead children on a picture walk through the book. Turn to page 3. Point out the teacher and the children in the class. On page 4, invite children to guess what the teacher might be saying. On page 6, ask children to describe what the boy is doing. Together, describe what is happening in the final scene. Ask children if they think this is the beginning of the play or the end, and why.

READ THE BOOK

SET PURPOSE Support children as they set a purpose for reading *The Play*. Suggest that children choose a character from the cover illustration to learn more about. Let them know that after they finish reading *The Play*, they will talk about what has happened in the story and why it happened.

STRATEGY SUPPORT: MONITOR AND FIX UP Remind children to think aloud and to use pictures to help them understand the words as they read. Model the process. For instance: "I don't understand how Nate can make a tree. Let's look at the illustration and see." Suggest that children read in pairs, thinking aloud and pointing out details in the illustrations to one another.

COMPREHENSION QUESTIONS

PAGE 3 Why do you think the children are raising their hands in this picture? *(Possible response: The children are raising their hands because they have something to say.)*

PAGE 4 What do you think the teacher is reading to Kate? *(Possible response: She is reading a script.)*

PAGE 6 Why is Nate making trees for the stage? *(Possible response: He is making trees for the stage because the class needs props for its play.)*

PAGE 7 What was this story mostly about? What might be a good title for the children's play? *(The story was about putting on a play. Responses will vary, but should draw on information from the book.)*

REVISIT THE BOOK

THINK AND SHARE

1. Possible response: They are putting on a play.
2. They make a horse mask.
3. Kate, Jake, Grace, Nate
4. Possible responses: The play is funny. They are proud of their children.

EXTEND UNDERSTANDING Discuss with children how the illustrations enhance the meaning of the story. Ask them to think about how the pictures match the words and think about other ways the book could have been illustrated.

RESPONSE OPTIONS

WRITING Have children write and illustrate an alternate ending to the story, imitating the sentence pattern. For instance: What could the parents do? They will smile and clap. Encourage children to read their pages to their classmates.

DRAMA CONNECTIONS Help children plan a performance of a favorite story to share with their classmates. Together, plan who will perform each role, who will help make the costumes, and who will assemble the props.

Skill Work

TEACH/REVIEW VOCABULARY

Write the vocabulary words on the board. Read the words together. Ask children to locate each word in the text and mark it with highlighting tape. Print the words on index cards and let children take turns selecting a card and saying it in a sentence.

ELL Invite English language learners to play a guessing game with vocabulary cards. Stack word cards facedown. Have children take turns selecting a card and making up a riddle about the spelling or meaning of the word for the group to guess.

TARGET SKILL AND STRATEGY

CAUSE AND EFFECT Point out to children that when they read a story, they can think about what happened (effect) and why it happened (cause). Provide an example: Drop a book on the floor and have children listen for the loud noise. Discuss how the noise occurred because the book was dropped. As children read *The Play*, ask specific questions to guide their thinking about what happens and why. Ask: Why did Grace and Jake make a horse? Why did the grownups come to the auditorium?

MONITOR AND FIX UP Remind children that what they read should make sense. Good readers ask themselves questions to make sure that they understand what they are reading. If they are confused about what is happening and why it is happening, they should look at the illustrations to help them understand.

ADDITIONAL SKILL INSTRUCTION

MAIN IDEA Display an illustration from a book the group has recently read and ask children to tell what the picture is all about. Point out that stories, just like pictures, are about something and that children can use their own words to tell what a story is about. After children have read *The Play*, turn back to selected pages and ask: What are these sentences mostly about? How can you tell?

Name_____

Cause and Effect

Read the sentences.
Circle the sentence that tells what happened.
Underline the sentence that tells why it happened.

1. Grace and Jake need a job to do. Grace and Jake will make a horse from old paper.

2. We need trees for the stage. Nate will make trees for the stage.

3. The play was funny. The parents smiled and laughed.

4. **Draw what happened.**   **Draw why it happened.**

Name_____

Vocabulary

Read the story.
Then circle the word that will finish each sentence.
Write the word on the line.

What could Kate do?
Kate will be a yellow bird.

What could Grace and Jake do?
Grace and Jake will make a horse.
They will cut old paper.

Words to Know

be   could   horse   old   paper

_____
----

1. What _____ Kate do?

could   are   make

_____
----

2. Kate will _____ a yellow bird.

been   by   be

_____
----

3. Grace and Jake will make a _____ .

horse   ham   hat

_____   _____
-----------------   ------------------------

4. They will cut _____   _____ .

big   old   paper   class

My Neighborhood

SUMMARY In this story, a girl takes us on a tour of her neighborhood. We see people who live and work there, different shops, and a park to play in. We also get on and off a bus and meet a police officer. At the end we realize that a neighborhood can be a busy place.

LESSON VOCABULARY

live	out
people	who
work	

INTRODUCE THE BOOK

INTRODUCE THE TITLE AND AUTHOR Cover up the book title, and encourage children to explore and describe the cover illustration. Have them conclude where this scene takes place. Confirm that it is a neighborhood. Reveal the title and ask children if they see the word *neighborhood*. Help them read the book title, as well as the author's and illustrator's names.

BUILD BACKGROUND Invite children to describe their own neighborhoods, or the school neighborhood. Elicit from children specific details about the people, buildings, and other physical features they see in the neighborhood. Summarize that a neighborhood is a place where people live, work, shop, and play.

PREVIEW/TAKE A PICTURE WALK Let children look through the art in the book. On each page, have children find the person who might be telling the story. Call attention to the buildings in the background of page 5, and ask children what type of neighborhood this might be. *(a city)*

ELL Use plastic toy figures to help children learn the vocabulary words. Gather a group of figures, and say, *"People."* Place the people inside a toy house, and say, "People *live* here." Use the figures to demonstrate and practice all words.

READ THE BOOK

SET PURPOSE Remind children that authors have a purpose, or a reason, for writing a book. Explain that readers can have a purpose for wanting to read a book, too, and encourage children to set a purpose for reading this book. For example, perhaps children are interested to know what the girl does for fun in her neighborhood. Tell children to look for the answers to their questions as they read.

STRATEGY SUPPORT: ASK QUESTIONS Remind children that asking questions as they read is a good way to clarify the text and confirm their understanding. Suggest that children pause after each page and ask a question to make sure they have understood what they have read. For example, after reading page 6, children might ask, "Where are the girl and her father?"

COMPREHENSION QUESTIONS

PAGE 3 Why does the author start the book with people? *(Because the people are interesting; because the people have fun jobs)*

PAGE 4 What question might you ask to help you understand this page? *(What game are they playing? What game uses balls and bats?)*

PAGE 5 Who might Mitch be? How do you know? *(A friend; usually you call friends by their first names.)*

PAGE 7 What can you tell about Ms. Whit's job? *(She is probably a police officer because she is wearing a uniform.)*

REVIST THE BOOK

THINK AND SHARE

1. Possible responses: The author wants to show that people make the neighborhood special.
2. Possible responses: What else is in the girl's neighborhood? Where is her school?
3. Possible responses: Many people live here. There is a lot to do in this neighborhood.
4. Possible responses: The neighborhood has some tall buildings. Different types of people live in this neighborhood.

EXTEND UNDERSTANDING Ask children to explain how this story ends, and agree that it ends with the girl and her father riding the bus. Encourage children to suggest places for where the girl and her father might be going. Prompt children to consider places in their neighborhood that might be in the girl's neighborhood too, such as a library, a mall, her grandparents' home, and so on.

RESPONSE OPTIONS

WRITING Have children copy the sentences, *This is my neighborhood. It is ___ .* Encourage children to complete the sentence starter with information about their neighborhoods. If time allows, let children draw pictures to illustrate their sentences.

WORD WORK Write the word *neighborhood* in the center of a word web. Then elicit from children words they associate with *neighborhood*, and write their words in the surrounding circles of the web. Encourage children to explain their word choices.

SOCIAL STUDIES CONNECTION

Time For SOCIAL STUDIES

Invite children to compare their neighborhoods with the neighborhood they read about in the book. You might set up a Venn diagram to help children record and compare ideas.

Skill Work

TEACH/REVIEW VOCABULARY

Write the word *people* on the board, and help children read it. You might point out that in this word, the letters *eo* make the long e sound. Have children use the word *people* with the other vocabulary words. For example: *People live in neighborhoods. People work in neighborhoods. Who are the people in our neighborhood?*

TARGET SKILL AND STRATEGY

AUTHOR'S PURPOSE Mention to children that the *author's purpose* is the reason why an author chose to write a story. Speculate why an author might choose to write about a neighborhood. For example, the author may want to show people what it is like where he or she lives. Tell children that as they read, they should try to figure out the author's purpose.

ASK QUESTIONS Share with children that when they read, it helps to ask questions about the text. Asking questions helps clarify information or parts of a story. For example, for this story, children might ask, "Why did the author have the girl tell the story?" *(The author wanted us to experience the neighborhood as she does.)*

ADDITIONAL SKILL INSTRUCTION

DRAW CONCLUSIONS Explain that when they finish reading a story, they should try to put together what the book was trying to tell them. As they do so, they should consider their own knowledge about neighborhoods. Help children draw conclusions about this story. First, invite children to recall the details of this neighborhood. Next, have children express their own ideas about neighborhoods. Finally, have them combine all their ideas into a statement.

Name _____

Author's Purpose

Look at the picture and read the words.

I play in this park.
I see lots of people.
This is a busy place.

Why do you think the author wrote *My Neighborhood*?
Use the words in the box to fill in the blanks.

> show   share   people   park

_____

1. The author likes the _____ .

_____

2. The author wants to _____ a busy neighborhood.

_____

3. The author cares about _____ in the neighborhood.

_____

4. The author wants others to _____ her neighborhood.

Name _____

Vocabulary

Complete each sentence with a word from the box.
The pictures will help you to fill in the blanks.

Words to Know
live   out   people   who   work

1. This picture shows _____ _____ .

2. People _____ in a _____ .

3. People _____ in a _____ .

4. _____ do you see here?

5. I like going _____ in my neighborhood!

We Look at Dinosaurs

SUMMARY A dinosaur expert looks at dinosaur bones to help decide what the dinosaurs ate.

LESSON VOCABULARY

down inside
now   there
together

INTRODUCE THE BOOK

INTRODUCE THE TITLE AND AUTHOR Discuss with children the title and author of *We Look at Dinosaurs*. Ask: Looking at the cover, where do you think the dinosaurs are? Is this a picture of a time like today or long ago? Turn to the title page. Ask: Where do you think this woman is?

BUILD BACKGROUND Have children share their knowledge of dinosaurs and any experiences of seeing fossils and dinosaur exhibits. Ask them if they think dinosaurs ate meat, plants, or both.

PREVIEW/TAKE A PICTURE WALK Invite children to look at the pictures in the book before reading. Discuss what children think is happening in the pictures. Point out that there is a thought bubble on page 4 that shows the woman is thinking about dinosaurs. Ask children to tell you what they think is going to happen to the bones on page 5. Ask them to tell the differences they see between the dinosaurs on pages 6 and 7.

READ THE BOOK

SET PURPOSE Have children set a purpose for reading *We Look at Dinosaurs*. Children's interest in dinosaurs should guide this purpose. Suggest that children think about what different dinosaurs might eat and how people can find out about dinosaurs.

STRATEGY SUPPORT: MONITOR AND FIX UP Remind children that as they read, they should always check to see if what they are reading makes sense and if they understand the information. If they don't know what a word means, or if it doesn't make sense in the sentence, they should go back and make sure they have read the word correctly. Tell children the pictures in *We Look at Dinosaurs* usually show the information that the words say. If they are reading something that seems very different from the picture, they should reread, or ask someone to help check the words.

COMPREHENSION QUESTIONS

PAGE 3 The people in this picture have just found some dinosaur bones. What do you think they will do with them? (*Possible response: put them in museum*)

PAGE 5 What is the woman's job? (*Possible response: to look at dinosaur bones and figure out what dinosaurs ate*)

PAGE 6 What is the big dinosaur on the page doing? (*Possible response: It is about to eat a tree.*)

PAGE 7 What do you think the dinosaur on this page is going to eat? (*Possible response: the little green lizard*)

PAGE 8 What on this page can help you understand what the words say? (*The picture can help.*)

REVISIT THE BOOK

THINK AND SHARE

1. First: plants; Next: meat
2. We look at the bones.
3. *We'll*
4. The reader should first point to the dinosaur on page 6 and then the one on page 7.

EXTEND UNDERSTANDING Ask children how having people in the same picture as the finished dinosaur model helped them to understand how big some dinosaurs were. (See page 8.) Then ask children which were their favorite pictures and have them explain why.

RESPONSE OPTIONS

VIEWING Make other picture books about dinosaurs available to the class. Invite children to look through the books and see many different kinds of dinosaurs. Have children write their names on small, self-stick note papers. Have children stick their names on different pictures of dinosaurs (one name per page). Call on each child to show his or her picture and tell whether the dinosaur would eat meat or plants and why.

SCIENCE CONNECTION

Display a variety of picture books about dinosaurs. Invite children to look through the books to see what different dinosaurs looked like and where they might have lived. Afterwards encourage children to describe the different dinosaurs.

Skill Work

TEACH/REVIEW VOCABULARY

Make vocabulary word cards. Have children pick a word when you call out that word's opposite. *(Up/down, outside/inside, here/there, alone/together)*

ELL To make sure children understand information in the text, have them point to pictures that illustrate the following words: *dinosaur* and *bones*. For the word *meat*, use pictures in classroom books to show different examples of meat.

TARGET SKILL AND STRATEGY

SEQUENCE Tell children that a good way to understand information in a book is to think about what happens first, next, and last. To help students better understand the information in *We Look at Dinosaurs*, write the following on sentence strips: *Seeing what the dinosaur looked like. Putting the bones together. Finding bones.* Then help children put the sentences in a sequence that makes the most sense. *(Finding bones, putting bones together, seeing what the dinosaur looked like.)*

MONITOR AND FIX UP Tell children that as they read, they should ask themselves if what they are reading makes sense to them. If it doesn't, they should go back and reread slowly. Tell children they should take the time to try to understand everything on a page before reading the next page. This will help them to better understand the information that comes next.

ADDITIONAL SKILL INSTRUCTION

CAUSE AND EFFECT Tell children that as they read they should think about what happened and why it happened. In *We Look at Dinosaurs*, people are looking at dinosaur bones. Note that the bones are displayed in a museum. Ask why the bones might be in the museum. Tell children that the bones being shown in the museum is what happened and why it happened is because people want to learn more about dinosaurs.

Name _____

Sequence

Think about *We Look at Dinosaurs*. Write 1, 2, and 3 to tell what happened first, next, and last. Draw a picture to show each step.

_____ Dinosaurs died.

_____ Dinosaurs lived.

_____ We study dinosaurs bones.

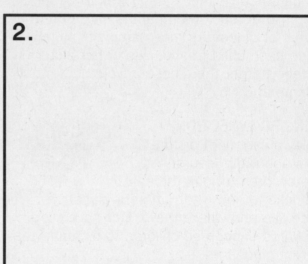

3.

Name _____

Vocabulary

Circle the picture that shows the word.

1. down

2. together

3. outside

Next to each word, write a sentence using that word.

4. there _____

_____

_____

5. now _____

_____

The Forest

SUMMARY Many plants and animals live in forests. In the fall, some leaves turn yellow and red. In this text, readers see the forest through the eyes of two children.

LESSON VOCABULARY

around	find	food
grow	under	water

INTRODUCE THE BOOK

INTRODUCE THE TITLE AND AUTHOR Read the title and the author's name, and invite children to read them with you. Write the word *forest* on the board, and say it several times with the group so they become familiar with it. Then discuss the images on the book cover, and ask children what shapes they see. Confirm for children that these shapes are trees. Speculate with children how the shapes might relate to the content of the book.

BUILD BACKGROUND Share with children that forests are places where plants and animals live. Invite children to predict what plants and animals they might see if they visited a forest. Ask: Do you think you will see in this book some of the plants and animals you have named?

PREVIEW Invite children to take a picture walk through this book. Encourage children to point out the first thing they notice. Many children might call attention to the shapes in which the photographs have been placed. Challenge children to identify the shapes they see.

READ THE BOOK

SET PURPOSE Help children set a purpose for reading, based on their own interest in plants, animals, or other things related to the topic. Encourage children to select a photo they might like to know more about.

STRATEGY SUPPORT: PREVIEW Model for children the strategy of previewing. Turn to page 3, and say, "I am going to preview the information I might find in the text. I see a forest, and I see two children. I think I will read the word *forest* in the text. When I read, I'll look for words and ideas I gathered when previewing." Invite children to read the text with you, then discuss how previewing helped prepare them for reading.

COMPREHENSION QUESTIONS

PAGE 3 Why does the author include two children in this book? (*Possible response: The author wants readers to see the forest as it is experienced by two children. The author hopes other children will want to visit a forest, like the children in the book.*)

PAGE 5 In which season do leaves turn yellow? (*in the fall*)

PAGE 6 Preview the article by looking at this picture. What words might we read in the text? (*Possible response: squirrel, nut, animals, forest*)

PAGE 8 If you watched birds in a forest, what might you see them do? (*Possible response: fly, sit on a branch, sing, look for food*)

REVISIT THE BOOK

THINK AND SHARE

1. Possible response: The author wanted to show readers that the forest is a fun and interesting place.

2. Possible response: We talked about the vocabulary words. We looked at the pictures. We predicted what we might see in a forest. We talked about and identified the picture shapes. This helped give an idea of what the book might be about.

3. *looked*

4. Possible response: Responses will vary but should include mention of trees or pictured aspects of the forest.

EXTEND UNDERSTANDING Work with children to make the connection between the shape on each page and the photograph within. For example, the shape on page 5 is a leaf; the photograph shows yellow leaves in the fall. Let children have fun suggesting other shapes and photographs that could be included in a book about forests.

RESPONSE OPTIONS

WORD WORK Say *forest*, and invite children to share words they think of when they hear this word. List words on the board. Circle words that appear in the book. Organize the words into groups, such as animal words, plant words, weather words, descriptive words. Conclude by asking children to draw and cut out leaf shapes. Have children write one word inside each leaf shape. Then arrange the leaf shapes or on the branches of a bulletin board tree titled, "A Forest of Words."

SCIENCE CONNECTION

Set up a Venn diagram, and label one side *Mammals* and one side *Birds*. Tell children that squirrels and bears are mammals, and ask children to list their physical features. Examples could include fur, four legs, can't fly, live babies. Then ask children how birds differ from mammals, and elicit ideas for the Venn diagram, such as feathers, wings, two legs, can fly, babies hatch from eggs.

Skill Work

TEACH/REVIEW VOCABULARY

Write sentences on the board for each vocabulary word. Say the word, then ask children to read the sentence and find the word in the sentence. Talk about the meaning of the word in the context of the sentence.

ELL Bring a plant to class, invite a child to water the plant, and say *water*. Using the plant as a reference, use gestures to help children understand the meaning of *around, find, food, grow,* and *under*. Have children repeat each word, imitating gestures.

TARGET SKILL AND STRATEGY

AUTHOR'S PURPOSE Explain that an *author's purpose* is the reason why an author chose to write something. Speculate with children why the author might have chosen to write this book. Let children exchange ideas; for example, this author may want readers to learn about a forest.

PREVIEW Share with children that previewing helps readers think about words or ideas they might read on the page. Have children turn to page 6 and look at the picture. Ask: Based on the picture, what words might you read in the text?

ADDITIONAL SKILL INSTRUCTION

CAUSE AND EFFECT Set up a tower of blocks on the floor. Roll a ball along the floor so that it knocks over the blocks. Invite children to describe what has happened and tell why it happened.
1. The blocks falling is what happened.
2. The ball rolling into the blocks is why it happened.

Help children discover a cause-and-effect scenario in this book. For example, on page 5: We saw trees with yellow leaves. Ask: Why did the leaves turn yellow?

Name _____

Author's Purpose

Look at the picture and read the sentences.

Many trees live and grow in this forest.

Many animals live and grow in this forest.

Why do you think the author wrote about trees and animals?

The author wanted to tell what lives in a forest. The author wanted us to know that a forest is a home to many plants and animals.

Use the words in the box to fill in the blanks.

$$\boxed{\text{show} \quad \text{trees} \quad \text{visit} \quad \text{forest}}$$

1. The author likes the _____ .

2. The author wants to _____ that animals live in the forest.

3. The author wants others to _____ the forest.

4. The author likes to look at _____ .

Name _____

Vocabulary

Use a word from the box to complete each sentence.

Words to Know
around   find   food   grow   under   water

1. Look! The bear is in the _____ .

2. He hopes to _____ food there.

3. He likes to eat fish. Fish are his _____ .

4. Fish swim _____ the water.

5. The trees _____ tall.

6. The bear looks all _____ .

Worker Bees

SUMMARY Worker bees are responsible for making honey. In this book, readers follow a worker bee as it leaves the hive and visits flowers to collect nectar and pollen. The bee then returns to the hive, where other bees feed the pollen to young bees and turn the nectar into honey.

LESSON VOCABULARY

also	family
new	other
some	their

INTRODUCE THE BOOK

INTRODUCE THE TITLE AND AUTHOR Have children study the words and pictures on the book cover. Ask children if one of the words names the animal they see. Have children point to the picture and say *bee,* then point to the word *bee* on the cover and read it. Read the entire book title with the class, as well as the author's name. Let children share their ideas about or experiences with bees.

BUILD BACKGROUND Show children a jar of honey and encourage them to react to it. Then ask children if they know where honey comes from. If they don't know, explain that bees make honey. Speculate with children how bees might do this, and write their ideas on the board.

PREVIEW/TAKE A PICTURE WALK Encourage children to leaf through the book to become familiar with the pictures and the graphic elements. Have children pause on pages 4 and 5, and discuss the shape of the pictures and why the shape might be important. Also have children finger-trace the arrows, and ask them what they think these arrows represent. *(a sequence)*

READ THE BOOK

SET PURPOSE Ask children why they might want to read this book, and list their ideas. For example, some children might want to know why humans need bees. Encourage children to think of something that people get from bees.

STRATEGY SUPPORT: PRIOR KNOWLEDGE Explain to children that they can use what they already know to help them understand what they read. Model text-to-self connections for page 3: "This reminds me of the honey jar I have at home." Model page 4: "The part about the bees going to the flowers makes me think about the bees I see in the park every spring."

COMPREHENSION QUESTIONS

PAGE 4 What is alike about the shape of the pictures and the shapes you see in the hive? What is different? *(Both shapes have six sides. The shapes of the pictures were made by people. The shapes in the hive were made by bees.)*

PAGE 5 What happens before the bees leave the flowers? What happens after? *(They get nectar and pollen. They return to the hive.)*

PAGES 6–7 Why do worker bees collect pollen and nectar? *(to feed new bees and to make honey)*

PAGE 8 What two things do worker bees do? *(They help make honey. They keep the hive working.)*

REVISIT THE BOOK

THINK AND SHARE

1. Responses will vary.
2. Responses will vary.
3. *bees, feed*
4. The arrows show that the bee leaves the hive and flies to the flowers.

EXTEND UNDERSTANDING Review with children their initial thoughts and ideas about bees that they shared prior to reading. Ask children how their ideas about bees differ now that they've read the book. Prompt children to explain why bees visit flowers and how bees help people. Let children point to pictures in the book to support their ideas.

RESPONSE OPTIONS

WRITING Prompt children to write about the worker bee from the worker bee's perspective. Have children copy and complete this sentence and sentence starter: *I am a worker bee. I _____ .*

WORD WORK Write the word *work* on the board, and encourage children to share images or adjectives that come to mind when they hear this word. Ask children if they think the term *worker* is appropriate to describe the bee in the book. Encourage children to explain their ideas by describing what the bee does.

SCIENCE CONNECTION

Speculate with children what would happen to the bees if no more flowers grew. Help children conclude that bees depend on the flowers. Ask: *Do the flowers depend on the bees?* Explain that bees help flowers to grow by taking pollen from flower to flower. Have children draw pictures of bees and daisies, then write titles for their pictures that explain this interdependency.

Skill Work

TEACH/REVIEW VOCABULARY

Give children sets of vocabulary word cards. Write each word on the chalkboard, then say the words in random order. Have children show each word as you say it.

ELL Show children a picture of an animal family, such as a dog with puppies. Write *family* on a self-stick note to place above the picture. Use the other vocabulary words to tell about the picture. Write and repeat the words, inviting children to say them with you. For example: This dog and her puppies are a *family*. The puppies are new. *Some* puppies have spots. *Their* fur is brown. This *other* puppy *also* has white spots.

TARGET SKILL AND STRATEGY

COMPARE AND CONTRAST Share with children that when they say how two things are *alike*, they tell how they are the same. When they say how two things are *different*, they tell how they are not the same. Have children *compare and contrast* the hive and the flowers on page 5. Ask: How are they alike? *(Bees spend time on both.)* How are they different? *(Flowers grow from seeds. Hives are built by bees.)*

PRIOR KNOWLEDGE Mention to children that they can use what they already know to help them understand what they read. Have children use a KWL chart for *Worker Bees* to generate questions for which they will look for answers as they read.

ADDITIONAL SKILL INSTRUCTION

SEQUENCE OF EVENTS Review with children that a *sequence of events* is the order in which things happen. Have children turn to page 4, and ask them which part of the illustration helps explain a sequence of events. Confirm that the arrows point to what happens next. Invite children to explain in their own words what is happening in this picture. Continue discussing the sequence as shown on each page.

Name_____

Compare and Contrast

Think about how you are different from a worker bee. Write a word on the line that that best fits each sentence.

Column A: You	Column B: Worker Bees
1. You live in a _____.	**2.** Worker bees live in a _____ _____.
3. You leave your home to go _____ to _____.	**4.** Worker bees leave their _____ hive to get _____.

5. Write one sentence that tells how you are similiar to a worker bee.

_____

_____

_____

Name_____

Vocabulary

Read the story. Think about the words in dark letters.
Then circle the letter of the answer to each question.

> Worker bees fly out of **their** hive. **Other** bees
> stay in the hive. They need to get **some** pollen
> from the flowers. They bring the pollen back to
> their **family** in the hive. The worker bees **also**
> help make honey.

1. What does the word **their** mean?

   a. belongs to it   **b.** belongs to them   **c.** belongs to you

2. What does the word **other** mean?

   a. different than   **b.** same as   **c.** one of

3. What does the word **some** mean?

   a. a lot of   **b.** not all of   **c.** all

4. What does the word **family** mean?

   a. two different animals   **b.** animals that live in a park

     c. a group of the same animals or plants

5. What does the word **also** mean?

   a. so   **b.** too   **c.** far

Nothing Stays the Same

SUMMARY In this fictional story, a young boy looks at his baby album and identifies the ways he has changed over time.

LESSON VOCABULARY

always	become(s)
day	everything
nothing	stays
things	

INTRODUCE THE BOOK

INTRODUCE THE TITLE AND AUTHOR Discuss with children the title and the author of *Nothing Stays the Same*. Ask: What does this title tell us about what might happen in the story? When do you think the story takes place?

BUILD BACKGROUND Ask children if they have ever seen pictures of themselves when they were babies. Discuss what the children looked like and what they did when they were very small.

PREVIEW Have children examine the cover of the book. Then have them turn the pages and look at the illustrations. Ask them to think about what the boy might learn in this story, based on what they know about growing up.

READ THE BOOK

SET PURPOSE Have children set a purpose for reading *Nothing Stays the Same*. Suggest that they think about something they want to learn. Think aloud: I see that the boy on the cover can do lots of things. I wonder what things do not stay the same. Does it mean his school or friends will change? I'm going to read and find out.

STRATEGY SUPPORT: PREDICT Predicting helps children set a purpose for reading and make sense of the text. As children make predictions about the book, encourage them to give reasons for their predictions. Prompt them to relate the text to what they already know. Ask, Why do you think so?

COMPREHENSION QUESTIONS

PAGE 3 Who is the baby in the photo album? *(The boy's baby pictures are in the photo album.)*

PAGE 5 What is the boy asking for? How does he ask? *(The boy wants some milk; he uses words.)*

PAGE 6 What did the boy eat when he was a baby? Does he eat the same food now? How can you tell? *(The picture shows the baby drinking from a bottle and the boy eating an apple.)*

PAGE 8 What are some other things the boy can do now? *(Responses will vary but should relate to the illustration.)*

REVISIT THE BOOK

THINK AND SHARE

1. Responses will vary but should relate to the examples in the book.
2. The boy will probably play ball.
3. *every, thing*
4. The boy looks at a photo album.

EXTEND UNDERSTANDING As children read the story, ask them to pay close attention to what the boy is doing in each of the illustrations. Discuss how the illustrations help tell the story.

RESPONSE OPTIONS

WRITING Ask children to write about something they can do now that they couldn't do when they were little. Encourage them to imitate the "When I was a baby, . . ." sentence pattern from the story.

SCIENCE CONNECTION

Suggest that children find out how their favorite animals grow and learn. Provide a selection of books and magazines relating to baby animals and their development. Encourage children to look for similarities and differences between animal babies and human babies.

Skill Work

TEACH/REVIEW VOCABULARY

Display the word *nothing* in a pocket chart. Read the word together. Then ask children to turn the pages of *Nothing Stays the Same* and find the word. Read the sentence aloud. Ask children to think of another sentence that uses this word. Repeat for the other words. Display the vocabulary words on a word wall.

ELL Show English language learners a book or magazine that contains photos of babies. Describe the babies and their activities. Focus on action words, such as *sleep, cry,* and *eat.* Then invite children to act out the words for their classmates to guess.

TARGET SKILL AND STRATEGY

COMPARE AND CONTRAST Point out to children that many things have changed since the boy was a little baby. As they read the book, suggest that children look for ways the boy has changed.

PREDICT Point out to children that as they read, it is a good idea to think about what might happen next in the story. Turn to page 5. The children will see a baby album here. There will be some pictures of the baby crying. As children read, prompt them to make predictions, using what they have read and what they already know.

ADDITIONAL SKILL INSTRUCTION

AUTHOR'S PURPOSE Ask: Why do you think the author wrote the book? What did he want to make us think about?

Name_____

Compare and Contrast

Think about when you were little. What did you do then? What can you do now? Draw a picture.

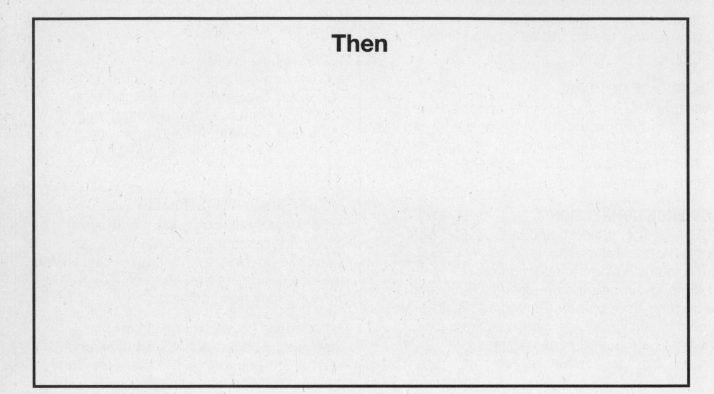

Then

Now

Name _____

Vocabulary

Read the words in the box. Write each word on the line.

Words to Know
always   become   day   everything nothing   stays   things

1. day _____

2. nothing _____

3. become _____

4. things _____

5. always _____

6. everything _____

7. stays _____

63

Can Hank Sing?

SUMMARY A bluebird, Hank, is frustrated because he cannot sing like his friend Jan. With practice and encouragement, he learns to appreciate his own unique singing voice.

LESSON VOCABULARY

any	enough
ever	every
own	sure
were	

INTRODUCE THE BOOK

INTRODUCE THE TITLE AND AUTHOR Discuss with children the title and the author of *Can Hank Sing?* Point out that the title is a question; ask children if they think the question will be answered in this story.

BUILD BACKGROUND Invite children to tell about a time they learned to do something new. Ask: Did you learn all at once, or did it take practice? Encourage them to recall their feelings at the beginning of the process and describe how those feelings changed as their skills grew.

PREVIEW/TAKE A PICTURE WALK As children preview the book, encourage them to look closely at the illustrations. Ask: Based on the illustrations, what do you think will happen in this story?

READ THE BOOK

SET PURPOSE Help children set a purpose for reading *Can Hank Sing?* They might concentrate on the story's plot, compare its outcome to the predictions they made while looking at the illustrations, or just think about how they would describe the story to a friend.

◉ SUMMARIZE Point out that a summary of a story is a short description of the characters and main ideas in a story. As children read, prompt them to ask themselves: What is the main idea on this page?

COMPREHENSION QUESTIONS

PAGE 3 How does Hank feel at the beginning of the story? How can you tell? *(Hank feels sad; the illustration shows him frowning.)*

PAGE 5 What does the speech bubble on this page tell us? *(The speech bubble indicates that Hank is singing in a small voice like a mouse.)*

PAGE 6 What about this illustration is a clue that this story is make-believe? *(Hank is sitting on a bench that is just his size.)*

PAGE 7 What did Hank learn in this story? *(Hank learned to like the way he sings).*

REVISIT THE BOOK

THINK AND SHARE

1. Possible response: In the beginning, Hank wishes he could sing like Jan. In the middle, he sings for Jan. At the end, Hank accepts his different way of singing.
2. Possible responses: 1. Hank said he could not sing. 2. Jan encouraged Hank and told him that his own way of singing was fine. 3. Hank sang. 4. Hank accepted his way of singing.
3. *bluebird*; *blue*, *bird*
4. Responses will vary but should be about a trait of the reader.

EXTEND UNDERSTANDING As children read the book, ask them to think about whether Jan was a good friend to Hank. Ask: Did Jan help Hank? How? How would you have helped Hank?

RESPONSE OPTIONS

SPEAKING Ask children to summarize the story in their own words. Prompt children to use transition words such as *first, then*, and *finally* in their retelling.

WORD WORK Make a word-and-picture puzzle card for the compound word *bluebird*. Sketch a blue spot and a bird on one side of the card and print the word *bluebird* on the other. Show the picture to the children and have them guess the word. Turn the card over and read the word together. Then invite the children to make word-and-picture cards for other compound words.

SCIENCE CONNECTION

TIME FOR Science

Help children use the Internet to locate the song of a real bluebird. Encourage them to compare the bluebird's song to those of other common birds.

Skill Work

TEACH/REVIEW VOCABULARY

Print each vocabulary word on a separate sticky note. Read the words aloud with the children and talk about the definition of each word. Then ask volunteers to match the words on the sticky notes to words in the book.

ELL Print the vocabulary words on word cards. Read them aloud, as a group. Then scatter the cards on the floor. Hand flashlights to one or two children. Call out a word from the list and let the children shine the flashlight on the corresponding word card.

TARGET SKILL AND STRATEGY

PLOT Point out to children that every story has a beginning, middle, and end. These events make up the story's plot. As children read *Can Hank Sing?* have them look for the beginning, middle, and end of the story. Suggest that they record these events on a story map. Encourage them to sketch pictures to help them recall the story events.

SUMMARIZE Point out that a summary of a story is a short description of the characters and main ideas in a story. Remind children that understanding the plot of a story makes it easier to do a summary. As children read, have them identify the main characters and the most important story events.

ADDITIONAL SKILL INSTRUCTION

REALISM AND FANTASY Discuss the difference between realism and fantasy. A *realistic* story tells about something that could happen in real life. A *fantasy* is make-believe. Read page 3 together and ask: Could this happen in real life? Encourage children to look for examples of fantasy as they read.

Name _____

Plot

Read the sentences. Put them in order. Write 1, 2, or 3.

_____   Hank likes the way he sings.

_____   Hank wishes he could sing like Jan.

_____   Hank sings for Jan.

Draw a picture showing how Hank feels at the end of the story.

Name _____

Vocabulary

Write a word from the box to complete each sentence.

Words to Know
any   enough   ever   every   own   sure   were

1. Hank and Jan _____ talking in the tree.

2. Jan said, "Almost _____ bluebird can sing like I do."

3. Hank asked, "Will I _____ learn to sing like Jan?"

4. Jan said, "If you practice _____, you can learn to sing."

5. Hank said, "Are you _____ ?"

6. Hank practiced _____ day.

7. In the end Hank liked his own _____ song.

A Big Move

SUMMARY In this story, a girl and her mother must move when her mother takes a new job in a different place. First, they begin to pack, and then they look for a home with a big yard near the school. Finally, it is time to say good-bye, but the girl hopes to make new friends.

LESSON VOCABULARY

away	car	friends
house	our	school
very		

INTRODUCE THE BOOK

INTRODUCE THE TITLE AND AUTHOR Have children study the book cover and explain what is happening in the picture. Ask children why the girl might be either putting her toys into a box or taking them out. When someone suggests that the girl is moving, invite children to read the book title with you. Also, read the author and illustrator's names. Ask children what *move* means, and make sure children make the distinction between moving their bodies and moving from one home to a new home.

BUILD BACKGROUND Share with children that sometimes families make the decision to move from one home to another. Sometimes the move might be in the same town, or very nearby. Other times, families choose to move to different states, perhaps even different countries. Talk with children about why a family might move, for example, to start a new job or to be closer to family members. If any child has recently moved to your community, you might invite him or her to share the experience, but be aware if the child is shy or does not feel comfortable speaking.

PREVIEW Invite children to preview the pictures in this book before they begin to read. Have children identify the people in this family, and agree that the family consists of a mother and a daughter. Tell children to turn to page 6, and ask them what the sign means in the picture.

READ THE BOOK

SET PURPOSE Guide children to set a purpose for reading. As they look at the book cover and think about the title, encourage them to voice what they would like to find out about this story. Jot down children's ideas. For example, perhaps children want to learn where the family gets the boxes. Tell children to look for the answers to their questions as they read.

STRATEGY SUPPORT: MONITOR AND FIX UP Mention to children that sometimes when they read, they form an idea about the text. When they reread the text, however, they may discover that they misunderstood what they read. Demonstrate monitoring and fixing up for the group. For example, read page 6 out loud, and then ask yourself, "Hmm. Who likes the big yard—the girl or the mother?" Then read the text again, and say, "Ah! The mother likes the big yard. I fixed what I misunderstood, so now I understand it correctly."

COMPREHENSION QUESTIONS

PAGE 3 Why do the girl and her mother have to move? (*The girl's mother has a new job.*)

PAGE 4 Why are boxes needed for moving? (*The boxes hold people's belongings, so they can take their belongings to their new home.*)

PAGE 5 Do the girl and her mother have a place to live yet? Reread the text to confirm your ideas. (*No, they must look for a house.*)

PAGE 7 What ideas do you have about the theme after reading this page? (*Possible response: When you move, you will miss old friends, but you can make new friends.*)

REVISIT THE BOOK

THINK AND SHARE

1. Possible response: People have to prepare for a move.
2. Possible responses: get boxes; pack things; look at homes that are for sale; say good-bye to friends
3. *boxes*
4. Possible responses: sad because I'm leaving my friends; excited to move to a new place.

EXTEND UNDERSTANDING Read with children the text on page 8. Have children apply what they learn here to the girl and her mother in the story. *(People may move close to home or far away, like the girl and her mom.)* Speculate with children how the girl might feel as she moves far away from her friends. Ask: Would you feel the same?

RESPONSE OPTIONS

WRITING Have children write a list of three things they would need to do if they had to move. Tell children to use information from the book or other ideas they have. You might have children copy and complete this sentence starter: *To get ready to move, you must _____.*

VIEWING Let children look through books that show pictures of various places around the United States. Encourage children to consider which of these places might be fun to move to. Have children share ideas about these places, based on the pictures in the books.

SOCIAL STUDIES CONNECTION

Time For SOCIAL STUDIES

Discuss with children why someone might move to their community. Have children suggest places in the community where new residents might work, live, shop, go to school, and have fun.

Skill Work

TEACH/REVIEW VOCABULARY

Give children vocabulary word cards. Then write these sentences on the chalkboard: *Some people live in a _____. Every day, we go to _____. My parents drive a _____. People I like are my _____. The cat ran _____ from the dog. I like cookies _____ much. _____ school is called....* Read each sentence, and have children show the correct word that completes it.

ELL On the board, draw a house, a car, and your school building. Label each picture with its vocabulary word, and have children say the words with you. Then have children draw a group of children they know, and have them label these children as *friends*.

TARGET SKILL AND STRATEGY

THEME Share with children that the *theme* of a story is the "big idea" or the lesson of the story. Suggest that children think about what we should learn from this story. Suggest that children consider how the characters act as they try to figure out the theme.

MONITOR AND FIX UP Instruct children to pause after they read each page and to consider what has happened so far in the story. To make sure they have understood everything correctly, tell children to reread the page and to revise, or fix, any misconceptions.

ADDITIONAL SKILL INSTRUCTION

CAUSE AND EFFECT Hold up a sheet of paper and rip it. Say, "I ripped the paper. This is a *cause*. Now I have two pieces. This is an *effect*." Explain that what happened is the *effect*, and why it happened is the *cause*. Read page 3, and ask children to explain in their own words what happened (the family has to move) and why it happened (Mom got a new job). Have children use a cause-and-effect chart to keep track as they read *A Big Move*.

Name _____

Theme

Look at the picture below.

What is the "big idea" of this picture?

Think about how the people in the picture feel.

Think about what is happening.

Write a few sentences to tell what you think.

_____
- -
_____
- -
_____
- -
_____
- -
_____
- -
_____

Name _____

Vocabulary

Complete the letter with words from the box.
Some words have pictures to help you.

Words to Know

away   car   friends   house   our   school   very

Dear Carlos, _____

We are moving! I am _____ happy.

We are not moving too far _____ .

I can still go to the same _____ .

I can still see my _____ .

We will put all _____ things

in the _____ .

We will then go to the new _____ .

I will tell you more after we move!

Your friend,

Mira

The Garden

SUMMARY In this story, a first grade class plants a garden and grows food to give to other people. It supports and extends the lesson concept that plants grow and change.

LESSON VOCABULARY

afraid	again
few	how
read	soon

INTRODUCE THE BOOK

INTRODUCE THE TITLE AND AUTHOR Discuss with children the title and author of *The Garden*. Say and ask: Look at the picture on the cover. Where are the children? Who is the man in the picture?

BUILD BACKGROUND Ask children to share what they know about planting a garden. Discuss reasons people might plant gardens: Do they want to grow pretty flowers? Do they want to grow vegetables to eat?

PREVIEW Have children look at the pictures in the book before reading. Where does the story take place? What do they think is going to happen in the book?

READ THE BOOK

SET PURPOSE Have children set a purpose for reading *The Garden*. Remind children of what they learned when previewing the book. Perhaps children might want to find out more about what kind of garden is being planted or why the children planted a garden. Let their own interests in gardening or working as a class help guide their purposes.

STRATEGY SUPPORT: VISUALIZE Discuss that the pictures in a book do not show everything that is happening. Children will have to use what they know about gardening and other things to better picture and understand what is happening. Model the strategy by telling children that you will picture in your mind what is happening in the cover art. Say: "These children are in a garden. I think I see the garden next to their school. I think I see them working in the garden. They are using gardening tools, and their clothes are a little dirty." Then, have children close their eyes as you read pages 4 and 5 aloud to them. After reading the pages, discuss the images that came to mind. Compare the illustrations in the book to what children visualized: What did they picture the children doing? Ask them to tell you how seeing the picture in their heads told them more than what is in the illustration: Did anyone besides Barb speak? Did the class vote? Did the class collect books to help them plan? Continue to have children stop and close their eyes to picture what is happening as they read. Pay particular attention to pages 6–7, where the plants develop over many days but the details are not discussed or shown in the book.

ELL To check understanding, have children explain what is happening in the illustrations.

COMPREHENSION QUESTIONS

PAGES 4-5 What happened after Barb said that the class should plant a garden? (*The class started to plan a garden.*)

PAGES 6-7 Why do you think nothing happened after the class first planted the seeds? (*It takes time for plants to grow.*)

PAGE 7 What do you think would be in a picture that came after this one? (*Possible response: children picking vegetables from the garden*)

PAGE 7 How do you think the children felt when their vegetables came up? Why? (*Possible response: happy; They are smiling in the picture.*)

REVIST THE BOOK

THINK AND SHARE

1. Beginning: Class planned a garden. Middle: Class planted the garden. End: The garden grew.
2. Possible response: First there was just dirt. Then tiny plants came up. The plants got bigger. Finally, vegetables grew on the plants.
3. *digging*; *dig* is circled
4. Possible response: They felt happy the plan worked.

EXTEND UNDERSTANDING Have children discuss everything that happened in the story. Is there anything else they would have liked to have happened in the story, or anything else that could have happened in the story? Invite children to retell the story using their own ideas for what else could happen in the story. Guide them to maintain a beginning, middle, and end in their retelling.

RESPONSE OPTIONS

SPEAKING Have children break into groups. Tell the groups that they should pretend they are each going to plant a garden. Working together, the members of each group should explain what they would want to grow in their gardens and why. Afterward, have one person from each group explain to the class the group's decisions about gardening as well as the reasons for their choices.

SCIENCE CONNECTION

TIME FOR Science

Display books that illustrate the life cycles of plants. Encourage children to look through the books. Afterward, have children pretend to be one of the plants they read about and describe how they would grow from seed to plant to being harvested.

Skill Work

TEACH/REVIEW VOCABULARY

Write each vocabulary word on the board. Then, make a set of cards with the following word or words: *scared, a second time, not many, in what way, see the words, before long*. Show and read the cards to children. Ask volunteers to say the vocabulary words that match.

TARGET SKILL AND STRATEGY

PLOT Tell children that a story has a beginning, middle, and end. As they preview the story, ask children to point out the beginning, the middle, and the end of the story.

VISUALIZE Say: "As you read a story, close your eyes sometimes and try to see pictures in your mind." Explain to children that this will help them find out more about what happens in the story than what the pictures show. Remind children that if they can picture what else is happening as they read the story, it will help them understand what happens in the beginning, the middle, and the end of the story.

ADDITIONAL SKILL INSTRUCTION

CHARACTER AND THEME: Remind children that characters are people or animals in stories. They can be real or make-believe. Point out that the characters in this story are the children in a class and their teacher. Tell children they can learn things about the children in the book by paying attention to what they do and how they feel. Looking at the pictures in the book will also help children to understand who the characters are and how they feel about gardening. Look at the beginning of the story. Who is Barb? Describe Barb. How does she feel about her plan? Do the other children like her plan? Then, ask children to tell you what they think the "big idea" of the story might be. After reading the book, revisit this question. Ask: What did you learn about people by reading this story? Does this story remind you of anything that happened to you in school or with your family?

Name_____

Plot

Think about what you read in *The Garden*.

1. Draw what happened in the beginning of the story.

2. Draw what happened in the middle of the story.

3. Draw what happened at the end of the story.

4. Now use your pictures to talk about the story.

74

Name_____

Vocabulary

Some of the following sentences use the wrong word from the box.

Put an X before any sentence that doesn't make sense.

Then, cross out the wrong word.

Write the right word at the end of the sentence.

Words to Know
afraid   again   few   how   read   soon

_____ **1.** I am soon the plants won't grow. _____

_____ **2.** I like to read books about plants. _____

_____ **3.** How can we grow food for others? _____

_____ **4.** There are very again seeds left. _____

_____ **5.** Soon the plants will grow. _____

_____ **6.** They had to use water afraid. _____

© Pearson Education 1

Animals Grow and Change

SUMMARY This informational text describes how different animals grow and change over time. The book begins with the familiar animals, cat and dog and then explores the growth and changes in others such as birds, gerbils, frogs, and butterflies.

LESSON VOCABULARY

done	know
push	visit
wait	

INTRODUCE THE BOOK

INTRODUCE THE TITLE AND AUTHOR Discuss with the children the title and author of *Animals Grow and Change.* Have children look at and identify the cover photographs. Ask: What do these pictures have in common with each other? What do you think you might learn about in this book?

BUILD BACKGROUND Engage children in a discussion of how they grow and change. Ask: How are you different now than two years ago? from when you were a baby? How do you think you might change in the future? If children have pets, ask how their animals have changed as well.

PREVIEW/TAKE A PICTURE WALK Have the children preview the book, looking at the pictures. Look specifically at the photographs on pages 4 and 5 and ask the children to describe what they see happening. Also encourage them to explore the other photographs and make predictions about the text.

READ THE BOOK

SET PURPOSE Based on your discussion of the cover photographs, invite children to share what about this text makes them interested in it. Ask: What animals would you like to learn about in this book? How do you think different animals grow and change?

STRATEGY SUPPORT: TEXT STRUCTURE Model for the children how to recognize the organization of written text. Ask children to tell what changes are shown on page 3. Also have them listen as you reread pages 4, 6, 7, and 8 aloud. Have children point out the sentence that is repeated on each of these pages. Help them to see the pattern that is repeated in the information about each animal.

COMPREHENSION QUESTIONS

PAGES 4–5 The text says that baby birds push out of eggs and later have feathers. Based on this information and photographs, do you think the birds can fly when they first come out of the eggs? Why or why not? (*No; Possible response: they need to wait until they grow feathers.*)

PAGE 6 How does the gerbil change over time? (*Possible responses: descriptions of size, closed/open eyes, amount of fur*)

PAGE 7 What are the different changes, in order, that this animal goes through? (*First, a tadpole; then it gets legs; last it changes into a frog.*)

PAGE 8 Look at the differences between each of these pictures. What does this tell you about the butterfly as it grows? (*Possible response: It goes through many different changes.*)

REVISIT THE BOOK

THINK AND SHARE

1. They also grow and change.
2. Pictures should mirror the photos on page 8.
3. *They, have*
4. It starts out as a tadpole, grows legs, and becomes a frog.

EXTEND UNDERSTANDING Call children's attention to the outside back cover of the book. Point out that this is a nonfiction book, meaning it contains factual information. Ask them to explain why this book is nonfiction, based on the information in the text. Also call attention to the "Science" label in the upper corner of the cover, and invite the children to share how this book is related to this content area.

RESPONSE OPTIONS

SPEAKING Ask children to describe the stages of a butterfly life cycle in their own words. Coach them in using the words *first*, *then*, and *last* to organize the sequence of events.

SCIENCE CONNECTION

Create a bulletin board. On one half, put the words *Animals change and grow* and invite the children to draw or help find photographs of baby and adult animals to put on the board. Label the other half of the board *We change and grow*. Invite the children to bring in two pictures of themselves: one current and one as a baby or younger child. Provide photos of yourself as well. Look at the board together and discuss the differences and changes you see in the pictures.

Skill Work

TEACH/REVIEW VOCABULARY

Create a set of cards with the vocabulary words printed on them. Create another set of cards with the following synonyms: *finished, understand, shove, stop by, stay.* Show each synonym card and read it aloud. Children can practice matching the correct words with the synonyms, saying the words as they do so.

TARGET SKILL AND STRATEGY

DRAW CONCLUSIONS Look at page 3 with the children and ask them to tell you what they see. Draw their attention to the arrows between the pictures and refer to the text to encourage the children to make decisions about the animals. Say: What does the information on this page tell us about the kitten and the cat? What about the puppy and the dog?

TEXT STRUCTURE Model for the children how to recognize the organization of written text. Using the information on page 8, assist children in writing the butterfly life cycle sequence in their own words, making sure to use the signal words *first*, *then*, and *last*. Have children go back and highlight or underline the signal words after they're done.

ADDITIONAL SKILL INSTRUCTION

SEQUENCE OF EVENTS Have the children turn to page 7 and look at the photographs. Ask them to describe what is happening as they refer to the photographs in sequence. Encourage them also to refer to the text for support.

ELL As you preview the book, invite English language learners to share the names of the young and adult animals in their home languages.

Name_____

Draw Conclusions

Draw a line from each set of facts to the correct conclusion.
Use *Animals Grow and Change* to help you.

A kitten has fur, whiskers, and a tiny cat body.

It will grow larger to become a grown-up cat.

Some animals change shape when they grow.

A caterpillar crawls at first.

It becomes a pupa.

It turns into a butterfly.

Some baby animals look like small grown-ups when they are young.

Name_____

Vocabulary

Circle the word that best completes each sentence.
Write the word in the blank.

one   wait   know
_____

1. Do you _____ what a butterfly is?

visit   crawl   done
_____

2. You are not _____ growing yet.

push   wait   know
_____

3. If you _____ long enough, it will get bigger.

one   visit   know
_____

4. Children _____ their friends after school.

crawl   done   push
_____

5. Friends can _____ you on the swing
to go higher.

Seasons Change

SUMMARY The weather outside is always changing. One reason why the weather changes is because of the different seasons. The weather begins to warm when it is spring, and the weather is mostly hot when it is summer. The weather begins to cool in the fall, and winter is the coldest time of all. This nonfiction text shows readers how the weather changes throughout the year.

LESSON VOCABULARY

before	does
good-bye	oh
right	won't

INTRODUCE THE BOOK

INTRODUCE THE TITLE AND AUTHOR Read the book title and author's name for the group. Point to each photograph and ask children to generate a list of words that describe the weather. Post the list in the classroom.

BUILD BACKGROUND Say the words *spring, summer, winter, fall* with the group, and ask children what these words stand for. Confirm that these words identify the seasons. Then invite children to talk about the seasonal weather where they live. Prompt discussion by asking, "How does it feel outside in the spring? in the summer? in the fall? in the winter?" Depending on where you live, you might explain that the change of the seasons and the weather can be more or less dramatic or obvious.

PREVIEW/TAKE A PICTURE WALK Invite children to begin looking through this book, and ask if they think this book will be a story or about something real. Ask children how they know, and agree that the photographs indicate that this book will tell them about something real;

this book is nonfiction. Then have children study specific pages, and ask them to predict which season they will read about on that page. Ask: Which season will we read about on page 6? How do you know?

ELL Pretend to walk away from the group, waving. Ask children what you should say when you walk away or leave, and have them all say *good-bye* with you. Make other hand or body motions for other vocabulary words, such as nodding your head for *right* (correct), making a surprised face for *oh*, or stomping your foot with your hands on your hips for *won't*.

READ THE BOOK

SET PURPOSE As children study the book cover and think about the book's topic, ask them what they would like to learn from this book. Start a KWL chart for the Prior Knowledge activity and record the children's ideas in it. Encourage children to look for their ideas as they read.

STRATEGY SUPPORT: PRIOR KNOWLEDGE Remind children that prior knowledge is the information they already know about a topic. As they read, encourage children to consider what they know about the seasons, as well as watch for the order of the seasons.

COMPREHENSION QUESTIONS

PAGE 5 Which season follows spring? *(summer)*

PAGE 6 What do you know about fall? How do the pictures confirm what you know? *(I know that leaves turn color in fall. The pictures show colorful leaves.)*

PAGE 7 How are trees in winter different from trees in fall? *(Trees in winter are bare. Trees in fall have colorful leaves.)*

PAGE 8 How do you think it would feel outside in the picture? *(It would feel cool and wet.)*

REVISIT THE BOOK

THINK AND SHARE

1. winter

2. Possible response: Spring is warmer than winter but still cool. Flowers bloom in spring. Leaves begin to grow.

3. *good-bye*; 4 times

4. Possible responses: It is raining, so the sky is probably cloudy and gray.

EXTEND UNDERSTANDING Share with children that the seasons occur not only in sequence, but in a cycle. The cycle, or pattern, repeats over and over again. To demonstrate what you mean, draw four circles on the board that form a circle, like the quarter hour positions on a clock (12, 3, 6, and 9). Connect the circles with arrows pointing clockwise. In the top circle, write *spring*. Ask children which season would appear in the right circle. *(summer)* When complete, help children conclude that the cycle of the seasons occurs over and over again.

RESPONSE OPTIONS

WRITING Invite children to write about their favorite season. Write the following sentences on the board for children to copy to jump-start their ideas: *How does it feel outside? It is _____. It feels _____.* Have them add at least one more sentence about that season.

VIEWING Ahead of time, find pictures that represent the seasons. Hold up the pictures and give children a moment to study the details. Then ask children to identify which season they see. You might also mix up the photographs and have children put them in the correct order.

SCIENCE CONNECTION

Talk with children about the clothes they wear during different weather and seasons. Describe the weather, and have children supply what they would wear. For example: *It feels cold outside! It is snowing. I should wear _____.*

Skill Work

TEACH/REVIEW VOCABULARY

Write each word on an index card, and display the cards in random order. Say the words one at a time, and have children identify the correct word on the card. Work with children to use the words in context in sentences.

TARGET SKILL AND STRATEGY

SEQUENCE Remind children that *sequence* is the order in which things happen. Suggest that children consider the order of the seasons as each is discussed in this book. You might ask children to say the seasons in sequence, then have them notice if the seasons appear in the same order in the book.

PRIOR KNOWLEDGE Share with children that *prior knowledge* refers to things they know before they begin reading. When they read, it helps to consider what they already know. This helps them to better understand what they read. Invite children to share what they already know about the seasons. Be sure to discuss the sequence of the seasons, too. You might list their ideas in the first column of a KWL chart.

ADDITIONAL SKILL INSTRUCTION

DRAW CONCLUSIONS Remind children that they can think about what they already know about seasons and put those ideas together with those they learned from the book to make new decisions or understanding about seasons. You may use these steps to help children draw conclusions.

• First, discuss with children what this book was mostly about.

• Then ask children what new ideas they formed from reading this book.

Name_____

Sequence

Read the name of the season in the first box.
Then write the name of the season that comes next.

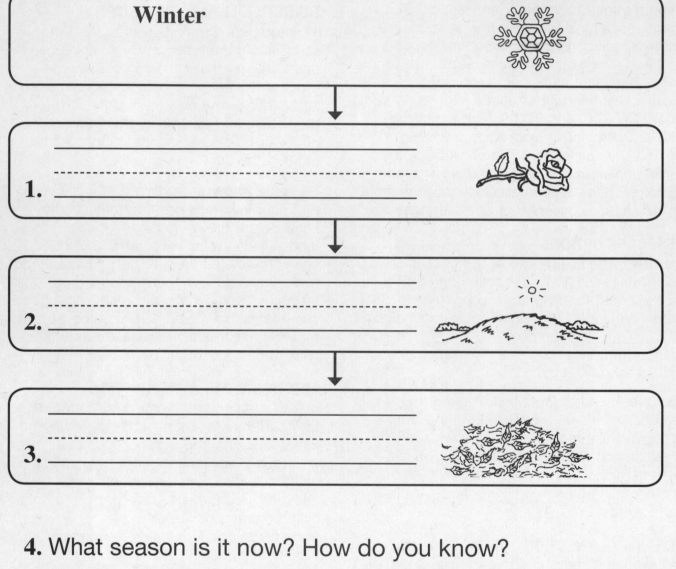

Winter

1. _____

2. _____

3. _____

4. What season is it now? How do you know?

_____

_____

Name_____

Vocabulary

Read the poem below, or listen as someone reads it to you. Look for the words from the box in the poem. Then circle the vocabulary words that you find in the poem.

Words to Know		
before	does	good-bye
oh	right	won't

How does it feel?

  Let's go outside.

Oh! It is spring!

  Let's wave good-bye—

To winter—won't

  you miss the cold?

It will come back,

  Or so I'm told.

You are right!

  Before you know it,

Winter is back,

  And it is snowing.

A Party for Pedro

SUMMARY Pedro's family is giving him a birthday party. They have a party that includes a piñata, tacos, and a band.

LESSON VOCABULARY

about	enjoy	gives
surprise	surprised	worry
would		

INTRODUCE THE BOOK

INTRODUCE THE TITLE AND AUTHOR Discuss with the children the title and the author of *A Party for Pedro*. Based on the title and the cover illustration, ask the children what special part of the party is shown. Talk about where the piñata game comes from and what that tells the reader about Pedro's family.

BUILD BACKGROUND Parties are a good way to learn about the music and food from different cultures. Ask the children to talk about different birthday parties they've been to and what was most fun about them. If they mention activities such as playing games together and eating special food, further the discussion by telling them they will be reading about one special birthday.

PREVIEW/USE TEXT FEATURES Invite children to look at the picture on page 7, and ask them what they think this book will be about. Then suggest they look through the rest of the book and figure out which character is Pedro. Ask: What do you think Pedro is celebrating?

READ THE BOOK

SET PURPOSE Most children will want to read about a party, but encourage children to set their own purpose for reading this story of Pedro's party. You can set the stage by stating that this is a story about a Hispanic family's birthday celebration. After the children have looked through the book, they should then be able to set a purpose for reading.

STRATEGY SUPPORT: MONITOR AND FIX UP Often, young readers think they are breaking the rules by going back to reread. Help children to understand that when you ask them questions and they don't know the answers, that's a clue that they should reread. It is important for them to realize that when they do not understand something they have a way for fixing it. This strategy will not only help the children's overall comprehension but also their ability to draw conclusions about what was important in Pedro's story. Remind the children that these strategies help them to think and read better.

COMPREHENSION QUESTIONS

PAGE 3 Why was the day special for Pedro? *(It was his birthday.)*

PAGE 5 What kind of game did the children play? *(a piñata game)*

PAGE 6 What food does Pedro's grandma make best? *(tacos)*

PAGE 8 Piñatas have been around what country for a long time? *(Mexico)*

REVISIT THE BOOK

THINK AND SHARE

1. Possible response: yes; he smiled and looked happy in the illustrations
2. Possible responses: You can reread, look at pictures, or keep reading to see if it makes sense.
3. Graphic organizer: birthday, wait, rain, plays, day
4. Grandma's candy, toys, treats

EXTEND UNDERSTANDING Have children turn to page 4. Point out the quotation marks, and remind children that such marks are used to show what a person actually said.

RESPONSE OPTIONS

SPEAKING Ask volunteers to prepare a short presentation of celebrations at their houses. They can include photographs, drawings, music, or any props in their presentations. Ask the audience to listen for similarities and differences.

SOCIAL STUDIES CONNECTION

Time For **SOCIAL STUDIES**

If possible, have any Hispanic children tell more about celebrations they have that mix their traditional culture with customs they know from their new country.

Skill Work

TEACH/REVIEW VOCABULARY

Write the vocabulary words on the board, say them, and ask the children to read them after you. Ask volunteers to use one or more vocabulary words in a sentence about parties. Repeat until all the words are used.

ELL Ask volunteers to tell about words in their home language that are good for describing parties and their activities. Encourage the children to describe parties in their home countries.

TARGET SKILL AND STRATEGY

DRAW CONCLUSIONS Model this skill by asking, after reading pages 3 and 4, "Why would Pedro ask if everything will be okay?" If necessary, prompt the children to remember that Pedro hopes to have a good birthday. Model a conclusion by saying, "It sounds as if Pedro hopes his birthday will be a good day."

MONITOR AND FIX UP It takes time for young readers to learn to monitor their understanding of what they are reading. One step in this process is to remind the children to use strategies, such as reread and review. Encourage them to ask themselves questions when they realize they didn't understand something. For example, they can ask themselves "Why doesn't this make sense?" Sometimes, they just need to continue and figure it out as they read.

ADDITIONAL SKILL INSTRUCTION

AUTHOR'S PURPOSE If children learn to ask why an author told a story a certain way or why the author put in some kinds of information, they will be closer to understanding what they are reading. In this story, ask why the author told about games, food, and music in Pedro's celebration. This way, the children will focus on how the author probably wanted to show this family's culture in the way they celebrate.

Draw Conclusions

What reason best fits each sentence.
Put the letter of your answer at the beginning of each sentence.

1. Pedro couldn't wait for this special day.

2. Everyone loved the music.

3. Pedro's Grandma makes a favorite food.

4. Pedro was surprised by the box his mother gave him.

5. Why was it a surprise to crack open the piñata?

A. Grandma's tacos are the best.

B. There were many toys inside.

C. Lots of treats fell out.

D. It was his birthday.

E. Everyone danced.

Name_____

Vocabulary

Read the story about Pedro. Put the word from the word box in the blank that best fits.

> **Words to Know**
>
> about   enjoy   gives   surprise
> surprised   worry   would

Pedro's story is _____ how

much he and his friends _____ his

party. Pedro does not _____ about

his family. They _____ all

_____ him and be there.

Pedro is _____ by all of the toys
inside the large box.

Reach for Your Dreams

SUMMARY When children arrive at Camp Dream, they are encouraged to acknowledge their special talents. Lee likes to cook, so he thinks someday he might become a great cook. Sam likes to draw, so he thinks someday he might become an artist. Jess isn't sure about her talent until she realizes that she is good at kicking a ball and can one day become part of a team. No matter their special talents or interests, all kids are told to reach for their dreams.

LESSON VOCABULARY

colors	draw	drew	great
over	show	sign	

INTRODUCE THE BOOK

INTRODUCE THE TITLE AND AUTHOR Point to the book title and read it with the class. Also read aloud the author's name. Then talk about what the word *dreams* means. Some children might say that dreams are pictures we have in our minds at night when we sleep. Also lead children to recognize that dreams are things we wish for or hope for the future.

BUILD BACKGROUND Ask children to think about people they admire, such as writers, artists, singers, even people in their communities. Talk with children about the talents each person has. Share with children that when people recognize their special talents, they can reach their dreams or goals of what they hope to one day become.

ELL Have children name individuals who are famous in their home country. Have them share with the class why these people are well known.

PREVIEW Encourage children to look through the book, noticing the art and the placement of the text. Have children study the pictures on pages 4 and 5, and have them identify the thought bubbles. Elicit that thought bubbles show us what someone is thinking or imagining.

READ THE BOOK

SET PURPOSE Ask children why they might like to read this book. Explain that when they consider what they hope to learn or get from a book, they are setting a purpose for reading. Prompt children to set a purpose for reading this book, for example, perhaps they would like to figure out what the images in the thought balloons on the cover represent. Tell children to look for the answers as they read.

STRATEGY SUPPORT: STORY MAP Remind children that a story map can help them keep track of what is happening in a story. You might suggest that children create a map that focuses on the characters in the book. Suggest that children write down each character's name and the dream he or she imagines.

COMPREHENSION QUESTIONS

PAGE 3 How does the name of the camp tie in with the book's theme? *(This book is about reaching for your dreams, and the camp is called Camp Dream.)*

PAGE 4 What information on this page can we add to our story maps? *(Dean likes to cook. He dreams of being a great cook one day.)*

PAGE 5 What do artists like to do? How do you know? *(Artists like to draw and make pictures. Sam likes to draw, and he wants to be an artist.)*

PAGE 6 What kind of team would Jess like to play on? How do you know? *(Jess would like to play on a soccer team. She likes to kick, and kicking is needed in soccer. She is kicking a soccer ball in the illustration.)*

REVISIT THE BOOK

THINK AND SHARE

1. Possible response: We all have special talents and dreams.

2. Possible responses: *Beginning*—Miss Jane asks the children to show what they like to do; *Middle*—Each child shows his or her special talent; *End*—Miss Jane tells the children to reach for their dreams.

3. Long *e*; *me, Lee, eat, being, team, each, read*

4. Responses will vary.

EXTEND UNDERSTANDING Have children look at the other figures in the illustrations, and lead them to notice details. Using these details, speculate with children what the dreams of these characters might be. Ask children if they think Camp Dream is an appropriate name for this camp, and have them explain why.

RESPONSE OPTIONS

WRITING Point out to children the images in the thought bubbles of the story characters imagining themselves achieving their dreams. Have children draw similar pictures of themselves. Encourage children to write captions for their pictures.

WORD WORK Write the word *dream* on the board, and let children share thoughts and ideas about the word that come to mind. Help children conclude that a dream could be something they have at night or a goal they wish for one day.

ART CONNECTION

Invite a local artist to speak to the group. Have the artist share what he/she thought he/she would be as a child when he/she grew up. Encourage the artist to explain how he/she reached his/her dreams.

Skill Work

TEACH/REVIEW VOCABULARY

Use the image on page 3 of the book to review the vocabulary words. Use the words in sentences that tell about the picture, and talk about the words' meanings.

TARGET SKILL AND STRATEGY

THEME Share with children that the *theme* of a story is the "big idea" or the lesson that readers learn from the story. You might share with children a well-known children's story and discuss its theme, such as the tale of the city mouse and the country mouse. Then encourage children to think about the theme of *Reach for Your Dreams* as they read.

STORY MAP Create a *story map* on the board for this book. Include boxes for the title, the setting, the characters, the problem, the solution, and the theme. Be sure to connect the boxes with lines to show the relationship between each story part. Then share with children that story maps can help them recognize the parts of a story. Have children copy the story map to complete after they finish reading and have discussed the theme of the book.

ADDITIONAL SKILL INSTRUCTION

REALISM AND FANTASY Write the words *Make Believe* and *Could Really Happen* on the board, and read them with the class. Point out that a *fantasy* is a story about something is make believe, and a *realistic story* about something that could happen in real life. Write the terms *fantasy* and *realistic story* under its corresponding description. Ask: Is a story about a girl who bakes cookies a fantasy or a realistic story? How about a story about a dog who bakes cookies?

Name _____

Theme

Look at the picture below.

What is the "big idea" of this picture?

Think about how the people in the picture feel.

Think about what is happening.

1.-3. Write a few sentences on the lines to tell what you think.

_____

- -

_____

- -

_____

_____

- -

_____

Name _____

Vocabulary

Write the word for each meaning on the lines.
Use the words in the box.

Words to Know
colors   draw   drew   great
over   show   sign

1. very good

_____

2. red, blue, yellow

_____

3. above

_____

4. make a picture

_____

5. to let someone see something

_____

6. something big with a message

_____

7. made a picture

_____

Dinosaur Bones Don't Rot

SUMMARY This informational book explains what happened to the dinosaurs when they died off and discusses the significance of dinosaur bones.

LESSON VOCABULARY

found   mouth
once   took
wild

INTRODUCE THE BOOK

INTRODUCE THE TITLE AND AUTHOR Discuss with children the title and the author of *Dinosaur Bones Don't Rot*. Focus children's attention on the content triangle on the cover. Ask: Why do you think this book is labeled *Science*? What information might be included in this book? Turn to the title page and ask children to compare the text on this page to the text on the cover.

BUILD BACKGROUND Ask children: How do we know that dinosaurs once lived on earth? Invite them to share what they know about dinosaurs and their bones. Show children a fossil (or a picture of a fossil) and discuss how the plant or animal might have become embedded in the rock.

PREVIEW/TAKE A PICTURE WALK Invite children to look through the book and preview the illustrations on each page. Turn to page 3. Ask children to describe what they see in the illustration. Turn to pages 4 and 5. Point out the arrows that show the sequence of decay. Ask: what do you think happened first? Next? Last? Turn to page 7. Ask: What are the people doing in this picture? Why do you think so?

READ THE BOOK

SET PURPOSE Help children set a purpose for reading *Dinosaur Bones Don't Rot*. Their interest in dinosaurs or questions generated while previewing the book should guide this purpose. Model choosing a purpose: I want to find out more about how scientists find dinosaur bones. I think I'll read this book.

STRATEGY SUPPORT: MONITOR AND FIX UP: Make available a children's dictionary so that children can look up unfamiliar words as they read. Think aloud as you model using a dictionary: I'm not sure what *museums* means. I think I'll look it up in a dictionary.

COMPREHENSION QUESTIONS

PAGES 4–5 Describe what is happening in each picture. Use your own words. (*Possible responses: An old dinosaur died and floated in the water. Its bones sank to the bottom of the water. Sand and mud buried the bones. The sand and mud turned to rock.*)

PAGE 6 Compare the illustration on this page to the illustrations on page 4. What is the same? What is different? (*The dinosaur bones are the same; the water is missing.*)

PAGE 7 The author of the book could have just told us about people finding dinosaur bones. Why do you think he told us about the dinosaur bones in the river? (*Possible response: He wanted readers to understand how the bones became buried underground.*)

PAGE 8 Tell one interesting fact you learned in this book. Why is it interesting? (*Responses will vary.*)

REVISIT THE BOOK

THINK AND SHARE

1. Possible response: The writer wrote the book to tell readers about dinosaur bones. He wanted us to learn where dinosaur bones come from.

2. Responses will vary but should contain information about two different dinosaurs.

3. *walked, died, covered, rotted, pushed, filled*

4. People are digging up the dinosaur bones.

EXTEND UNDERSTANDING Ask children to take another look at the illustrations on pages 4 and 5. Discuss what is happening in each picture. Together, make up a caption for each picture. Print the captions on sticky notes and attach them to the pages.

RESPONSE OPTIONS

WRITING Invite children to write a few sentences describing what they would do if they found a dinosaur bone. Provide art materials and have them illustrate their sentences.

SCIENCE CONNECTION

TIME FOR Science

Have on hand an assortment of reference books about dinosaurs. Suggest that children choose one dinosaur to learn more about. Encourage them to share what they learn with their classmates.

Skill Work

TEACH/REVIEW VOCABULARY

Write the word *found* on a sentence strip. Ask: What does *found* mean? What is the opposite of *found*? Turn to page 3 and ask a volunteer to find the sentence containing the word. Read the sentence together, and talk about the meaning of the word in context. Repeat this exercise for the words *mouth* (page 4), *once, took* (page 7), and *wild* (page 3). If a vocabulary word has no opposite, ask: What other words does this word go with?

ELL Print each vocabulary word on an index card. Stack the cards face down in a pile. Have children take turns picking a card and making up a riddle for others to guess. Riddles might include: *This word starts with the letter____.* Or *This word means the opposite of _____.*

TARGET SKILL AND STRATEGY

AUTHOR'S PURPOSE Point out to children that thinking about why the author wrote a book can help a reader understand the book. As children preview *Dinosaur Bones Don't Rot*, ask: What do you think the author wants us to know? Why do you think so? After the children have read the book, discuss some of the author's choices. Ask: Why, do you think, the author told us about what happened to a dinosaur after it died?

MONITOR AND FIX UP Remind children that what they read should make sense. When they encounter a word they don't know, finding out what the word means can help them understand what they read. They can look the word up in the dictionary.

ADDITIONAL SKILL INSTRUCTION

CAUSE AND EFFECT Remind children that when they read, they can think about what happened and why it happened. Turn to page 6. Read the paragraph and ask: Why did the land get higher? Guide children to understand that the land rose because the stream went dry.

Name _____

Author's Purpose

Sue's Skull

Think about why the author wrote this book. Read each question below. Then circle the best answer.

1. Why does the author tell us about dinosaur bones?

  a. to make us happy   **b.** to make us read   **c.** to help us learn

2. Why does the author tell us about how dinosaurs rot?

  a. to gross us out   **b.** to help us understand   **c.** to scare us
                                 more about dinosaurs

3. Why does the author show us bones coming out of the ground?

  a. to show how ugly   **b.** to show how   **c.** to get us to bury
     they are   bones are found   the bones

4. Why does the author tell us that people took the bones to museums?

  a. to get us to stay away   **b.** to get us to go to the   **c.** to bore us
     from museums   museums

5. Why did the author write this book?

  a. to teach us about   **b.** to make us laugh   **c.** to dig up bones
     dinosaurs

Name _____

Vocabulary

Words to Know
found   mouth   took   once   wild

Find each word in the box and circle it.

```
X  H  Y  P  W  V  T  I  L
L  M  O  U  T  H  O  N  I
D  N  H  G  G  D  O  E  H
V  H  D  L  T  N  K  M  J
O  T  C  B  C  Q  D  C  F
N  N  M  A  U  W  X  K  N
C  L  K  K  B  U  R  X  D
E  V  V  F  O  U  N  D  H
F  T  O  C  P  W  I  L  D
```

The Moon Festival

SUMMARY Mai looks forward to her family's celebration of the Chinese Moon Festival—especially the moon cakes.

LESSON VOCABULARY

above   eight

laugh   moon

touch

INTRODUCE THE BOOK

INTRODUCE THE TITLE AND AUTHOR Discuss with children the title and author of *The Moon Festival*. Direct children to look at the cover and notice what the girls in the picture are doing. Ask: Based on the picture and the title, what is one thing that might happen in this story?

BUILD BACKGROUND Invite children to discuss family celebrations. Ask them to share the names of some holidays that their families observe and talk about what traditions they follow. Also ask children to share what they know about China. Help children locate China on a map. Explain to children that they will be reading about a holiday celebration that started in China.

PREVIEW Lead children in a picture walk through the book. Turn to the title page and point out that the title of the book and names of the author and illustrator always appear on this page. Turn to page 3, and explain that the girl is named Mai and this is her mother. Ask: Where do you think Mai's mother has been? Turn to pages 4 and 5, and ask children to describe the action in the illustrations. Think aloud: "I wonder what the mother and daughter are cooking. It looks like they might be getting ready for a party." Turn to pages 6 and 7 and ask: What do you think the man is saying?

READ THE BOOK

SET PURPOSE Guide children as they set a purpose for reading *The Moon Festival*. Suggest that they reflect on the questions and predictions that arose as they previewed the illustrations. Think aloud: I wonder what the people in this story are eating. I think I'll read and find out.

STRATEGY SUPPORT: MONITOR AND FIX UP Encourage children to think aloud as they read. If they encounter a confusing section, suggest that they read on for clarification. Model: "I've never heard of moon cakes. I think I'll read on and see if the author explains what they are later in the story." Then have children practice using the strategy as they read *The Moon Festival*.

COMPREHENSION QUESTIONS

PAGE 3 Do you think Mai knows what the Moon Festival is? Why or why not? *(Possible responses: Yes, Mai knows what the Moon Festival is; she knows that there will be moon cakes.)*

PAGE 5 Does your family ever have celebrations like this? When? *(Responses will vary but should relate to children's personal experience.)*

PAGE 7 How did Mai know her wish would soon come true? *(The moon cakes were already on the table.)*

PAGE 8 Do you think this story could really happen? Why or why not? *(Possible responses: Yes, this story could happen. Families do celebrate holidays and have special dinners.)*

REVISIT THE BOOK

THINK AND SHARE

1. Possible response: Yes; the children are excited about this festival just as real children would be.
2. Possible response: I could go to the library and look for a book about the Moon Festival or look on the Internet.
3. Responses will vary.
4. Possible responses: Moon Festival: Eat moon cakes; Thanksgiving: Eat turkey; Both: Families gather together.

EXTEND UNDERSTANDING Invite children to study the illustrations and discuss the setting of the story. Ask: Do you think this story is happening now, or did it happen a long time ago? How can you tell?

RESPONSE OPTIONS

WRITING Ask children to think about what they would do if they could make a wish to the lady who lived in the moon. Invite them to write and illustrate a few sentences about their Moon Festival wish.

SOCIAL STUDIES CONNECTION

Time For
SOCIAL STUDIES

Encourage children to find out more about the Moon Festival. Provide a selection of nonfiction and fiction books about the holiday, and help children use the Internet to research Moon Festival customs.

Skill Work

TEACH/REVIEW VOCABULARY

List the vocabulary words on the board or on chart paper: *above, eight, laugh, moon, touch*. Ask children to read, write, and spell each of the words. Print each word on an index card. Have children take turns choosing a card, reading the word, and finding the word in the book.

ELL Introduce the word *festival* to Spanish-speaking students. Highlight the similarity between this word and *fiesta*.

TARGET SKILL AND STRATEGY

REALISM AND FANTASY Point out to children that stories can be *realistic* or *fantasy*. A *realistic story* tells about something that could happen in real life. Even though the story is made up, the events could really happen. The characters say and do things that real people can do. A *fantasy* is make-believe. In a fantasy, people do impossible things, animals talk, and so forth. Together, think of examples of both kinds of stories. As children discuss The Moon Festival, ask: Do you think that this story could really happen or is it make-believe? What makes you think so?

MONITOR AND FIX UP Remind children that what they read should make sense. They should ask themselves questions as they read. If they are confused by something they read, or aren't sure if a story is real or make-believe, it can be helpful to keep reading. Often, the answers to questions can be found further on in the text.

ADDITIONAL SKILL INSTRUCTION

PLOT Point out to children that every story has a beginning, middle, and end. Identifying the most important parts of a story can help them understand what they are reading. Draw a story map on the board, and ask children to help fill in the beginning, middle, and ending event.

Realism/Fantasy

Draw two pictures about a moon festival.
Show one thing that could really happen.
Show one thing that is make-believe.

Real

Make-Believe

Name _____

Vocabulary

Pick a word from the box to finish each sentence.
Write it on the line.

Words to Know
above   eight   laugh   moon   touch

1. Mother bought _____ round cakes.

2. Each cake looked like a round _____ .

3. "Don't _____ the cakes," said Mother.

4. The moon shone high _____ us in the sky.

5. Mai's silly wish made her _____ .

A Good Big Brother

SUMMARY A young boy worries about the arrival of a new baby but ends up liking being a big brother.

LESSON VOCABULARY

picture	remember
room	stood
thought	

INTRODUCE THE BOOK

INTRODUCE THE TITLE AND AUTHOR Discuss with children the title and author of *A Good Big Brother.* Based on the title, what do children think the story might be about? Who might the big brother in the story be?

BUILD BACKGROUND Encourage children to discuss any experience they have with the arrival of a new sibling. If they don't have personal experience, suggest they imagine how they would feel if they got a new baby brother or sister.

PREVIEW Before reading, have children look at the pictures in the book. Who do they think the people in the story are? What are the people doing?

ELL Check children's understanding of such words as *thought* and *remember.* Discuss the meanings of words, give examples of each in a sentence. Then have children give their own examples.

READ THE BOOK

SET PURPOSE Have children set a purpose for reading *A Good Brother.* Help prompt a purpose by exploring the following: What do children hope to find out about the family on the cover? Why is the book called *A Good Big Brother?*

STRATEGY SUPPORT: STORY STRUCTURE Help children to see that structure is something separate from content. As a class, make up a story about a child who wants a pet cat. Make sure the story has a beginning, middle and end. Then put the information in a story chart. Afterward, challenge children to create different beginnings. Continue creating the new story, guiding children to see that different beginnings might make different middles and ends, but the basic story structure (beginning, middle, end) does not change. When children have finished reading *A Good Big Brother* have them tell you the beginning, middle, and end of that story.

COMPREHENSION QUESTIONS

PAGE 4 Think about the questions Marco is asking. Why is he asking them? *(Possible response: He is worried about the new baby changing everything.)*

PAGES 5–6 How do you think Marco feels about sharing his room? *(Responses will vary.)*

PAGE 6 Look at Marco's room. Does it look like it could be a real room or not? *(Responses will vary.)*

PAGE 7 How does Marco feel about the baby at the end of the story? *(Possible Response: He likes the baby.)*

REVISIT THE BOOK

THINK AND SHARE

1. Marco is the boy in the story. Parents and the new baby brother are other characters.
2. Responses will vary but should include: At first, he is worried he won't like having a baby brother around; He's a good big brother. He shares his room and his dad's lap.
3. Sentences will vary.
4. Responses will vary.

EXTEND UNDERSTANDING Discuss how everything in this story could really happen. Then invite children to think of ways to turn this into a make-believe story. Help them to make sure the new story has a beginning, middle, and end.

RESPONSE OPTIONS

VIEWING Point out the family picture on the cover of *A Good Big Brother.* Then, have kids draw their own family picture.

SOCIAL STUDIES CONNECTION

Time For SOCIAL STUDIES

Display books that show a variety of family types (single parent, many children, single child, adoptive families, extended families, etc.). Give children the opportunity to look through the books and talk about the different kinds of families they see.

Skill Work

TEACH/REVIEW VOCABULARY

Write the vocabulary words on index cards. Have children take turns choosing cards and then using the word in a sentence.

TARGET SKILL AND STRATEGY

CHARACTER, SETTING, AND PLOT Tell children that *characters* are people or animals in stories. Then say that the main character in *A Good Big Brother* is a boy named Marco, who is worried about what might happen when his family has a new baby. Tell children that if they think about how they would feel with a new baby coming into their family, it might help them to better understand Marco. Also, ask children to think about the places they see in the pictures and why those places are important to Marco.

STORY STRUCTURE Remind children that all stories have a beginning, middle, and end. To help preview the structure of events in *A Good Big Brother* have children put the following sentences in time order: The baby comes; finding out there will be a new baby; getting ready for the new baby to come. Have children suggest how Marco might feel about each event. After reading, discuss which predictions were correct.

ADDITIONAL SKILL INSTRUCTION

REALISM AND FANTASY Ask children if a story where a boy finds a coat that makes him invisible is real or make-believe. Ask: Could this really happen? Have children explain their answers. Invite children to give you examples of stories where make-believe things happen. Then, ask children if a story where a boy finds a coat, returns it to its owner, and gets a reward is real or make-believe. Ask: Could this really happen? Have children explain their answer. Tell children that as they read, they should decide if the story could really happen or if it is make-believe. After reading, discuss their opinions.

Name _____

Character, Setting, Plot

In the boxes below, draw something that happened in the beginning, middle, and end of *A Good Big Brother*. Under each picture, write a sentence about who is in the picture and what they are doing.

Name _____

Vocabulary

Find the following hidden words. Words can go across or down.
When you have found a word, write it on the line below the puzzle.

Check the Words You Know

picture	remember	room	stood	thought

```
J H Y P O T E T J Y E C W Y
K L O I C R Y R M M S L U P
S A R C D L K T H O U G H T
D J I T E U D M Y P S P C R
T L O U Y A N D P O T Y F I
A P P R E L R E M E O T E R
I L T E T A N T Y P O R O M
T Y L V T Y I L E V D M K I
R E M E M E B E R S H A N E
K I U L S T R O O Z P I C T
U V W J A V I R O O M Y P L
```

1. _____   4. _____

2. _____   5. _____

3. _____

Does a Babysitter Know What to Do?

SUMMARY This nonfictional reader tells the story of a boy whose mother has to go to work and leave him with a babysitter. At first, he is unsure about the sitter and doesn't believe the sitter will know what to do. But his mother reassures him that the babysitter is good, that he will have fun, and that she will return home soon.

LESSON VOCABULARY

across	because
dance	only
opened	shoes
told	

INTRODUCE THE BOOK

INTRODUCE THE TITLE AND AUTHOR Ask children to look at the front cover of the reader. Read with them the title of the book, and the author's name. Ask what they think the book is going to be about, based on the title and picture on the cover.

BUILD BACKGROUND Ask children if they have ever had a babysitter. If they have, ask them if they liked their babysitters and why. If they haven't, ask them if they think it would be nice to have a babysitter. Also, ask children to name some of the reasons why parents sometimes need to hire babysitters.

PREVIEW/ILLUSTRATIONS Invite children to open the book and take a *picture walk* through the book. Then ask: Does this story look like it could really happen? Also ask: Who do you think are the main characters in the story? Ask the children to explain what clues led them to their answers.

READ THE BOOK

SET PURPOSE After children have previewed the book, ask them what question(s) they want to be able to answer after they read the book. Ask if there are any questions they have about the characters in the story. Point out that the title of the reader is a question.

STRATEGY SUPPORT: PREVIEW Remind children that a book's title is there to help them know what a book is going to be about. Remind children that illustrations are there to help them understand the words on each page. Invite the children to look at the illustration on page 4, and then ask them to point out which thought bubble goes with what sentence on the same page.

COMPREHENSION QUESTIONS

PAGE 3 Why does the boy's mom have to leave? *(She has opened a store and has to go to work.)*

PAGE 3 Where does the babysitter live? *(in the boy's neighborhood)*

PAGE 4 What is the boy worried about? *(He is worried that the babysitter won't know how to take care of him.)*

PAGE 5 Why does the boy want to put on his shoes? *(He wants to go with his mom rather than stay at home with a babysitter.)*

PAGE 6 Why does the boy change his mind about the babysitter? *(His mom tells him the babysitter will play any game he wants.)*

REVISIT THE BOOK

THINK AND SHARE

1. His mom is going to work.
2. Look at the pictures and read the title.
3. Responses will vary. She started a new business.
4. It can be fun.

EXTEND UNDERSTANDING Discuss with children the use of thought bubbles in illustrations. Direct children to the cover illustration, and emphasize how much information can be communicated through pictures. Have children interpret again what the cover illustration is conveying.

RESPONSE OPTIONS

SPEAKING Invite children to tell a story from their own lives that includes a cause and effect. Explain that the word *because* might be helpful. Give the children an example from your own life. (Example: I walked to school today because the weather was nice.)

SCIENCE CONNECTION

Develop an in-class science project that shows cause and effect. One possibility is to plant seeds, water them, give them light, and monitor the plants' growth. Ask students to list the causes and the effect.

Skill Work

TEACH/REVIEW VOCABULARY

Write the vocabulary words on the board. Help children find the words in the book. Guide them in reading the sentences that contain the words, and ask children to tell what they think each word means.

ELL Ask English learners to write the vocabulary words on homemade word cards. Encourage them to write the word in their home language, if it will aid their comprehension. Then ask the children to draw pictures to illustrate what they mean on the other side.

TARGET SKILL AND STRATEGY

CAUSE AND EFFECT Explain to children that a *cause* is something that happens, and an *effect* is something that happens as a result of the cause. (Examples: Cause: You spend the whole day playing in the hot sun; Effect: You get a sunburn. Cause: There is a very bad snow storm; Effect: There is a "snow day" and school is cancelled.) Ask children to draw a line down the middle of a sheet of paper. Then ask them to draw one picture on each side of the line: one picture for the cause and one for the effect. Invite children to draw pictures of something that has happened to them or someone they know.

PREVIEW Ask children what different feelings are portrayed in the two illustrations on the cover and on page 8. Based on those two illustrations, ask the children to think of a *preview* question they hope to answer by reading the book. (Example: Is the boy still worried at the end of the story?)

ADDITIONAL SKILL INSTRUCTION

MAIN IDEA Remind children that the main idea of a book is the most important thing the author wanted them to learn from the book. After reading the book, guide children in identifying the main idea.

Name _____

Cause and Effect

The sentences on the left tell a **cause**.
The sentences on the right tell an **effect**.
Draw a line to match each cause with its effect.

---

1. A mom goes to work.

2. It is time for a nap.

3. Mom comes home from work.

4. It is lunchtime.

5. You asked the babysitter to play a game.

a. The babysitter leaves.

b. The babysitter makes lunch.

c. A babysitter is coming to stay.

d. The babysitter tucks you into bed.

e. The babysitter plays a game.

Name _____

Vocabulary

Say each word aloud to count the number of syllables. Write that number on the line.

1. across   How many syllables? _____

2. because   How many syllables? _____

3. dance   How many syllables? _____

4. only   How many syllables? _____

5. opened   How many syllables? _____

6. shoes   How many syllables? _____

7. told   How many syllables? _____

8–10. Draw a picture of a person walking *across* something.

What the Dog Saw

SUMMARY In this story, a dog observes how different animals gather food.

LESSON VOCABULARY

along	behind
eyes	never
pulled(ing)	toward

INTRODUCE THE BOOK

INTRODUCE THE TITLE AND AUTHOR Discuss with children the title and author of *What the Dog Saw*. Also have children look at the picture on the cover. Ask what they think the book is going to be about based on the title and picture on the cover.

BUILD BACKGROUND Ask children to share what they know about how animals get food. Ask: Have you ever seen squirrels or birds gather food? How do they do it?

PREVIEW/TAKE A PICTURE WALK Have children look at the pictures in the book before reading. Ask: Who is the story about? Where does the story happen? Where does the story begin? Where does it end? Have children read the heading for the background information on page 8. Ask and discuss: Is this part of the story? What is this part of the book about? Why did the author include this information?

READ THE BOOK

SET PURPOSE Have children set a purpose for reading *What the Dog Saw*. Remind children of what they discussed when the title, author, and cover art were introduced. You may need to work with children to have them set their own purpose. Ask: Would you like to know what the dog saw?

STRATEGY SUPPORT: STORY STRUCTURE Remind children that stories are arranged in an order from beginning to end. Each thing that happens in the story leads to the next thing that happens. When they think about how all these events fit together, they can tell what the story is all about. Tell children that as they read *What the Dog Saw*, they will see that something happens over and over again. Encourage children to watch out for this pattern as they read the story. To help children discover the story structure, give children a graphic organizer with five boxes. Label the first box *First*, the next three boxes *Next*, and the last box *Last*. As they read, have children fill in each box by writing or drawing what happens after reading each page of the story. Ask: What happens more than once in the story? What is the story all about? Guide children to see that Brown observed a series of animals gathering food. This should lead children to see that the story is about how different animals get food.

ELL Give each child a two-column problem/solution chart. In the Problems column, list the following: hungry squirrel, hungry ant, hungry bird, hungry dog. For each problem, have children draw the food that was the solution for each animal in the story.

COMPREHENSION QUESTIONS

PAGE 3 On this page, Brown is talking to you, the reader. Do you think that could really happen or is it make-believe? Why? (*It is make-believe because dogs can't talk in real life.*)

PAGE 4 Where was the squirrel? (*in Brown's yard behind the house*)

PAGES 4–6 Which animal did Brown see first, next, and last? (*First: squirrel, next: ant, last: bird*)

PAGES 4–7 Which picture is the most like real life? Why? (*Possible response: The picture on page 7 because it looks like the way a dog eats food. In the other pictures, the squirrel has too*) *many nuts, the ant is too big, and the bird is carrying an apple as big as it is.)*

PAGE 7 Draw a picture of how the character Brown felt at the end of the story. *(Picture should depict Brown as being happy.)*

REVISIT THE BOOK

THINK AND SHARE

1. in the yard behind the house
2. Possible response: Brown sees the other animals trying to gather food. Squirrel: gathers nuts, Ant: pulls a pear, Bird: carries an apple
3. the ant
4. Possible response: People give Brown food. The other animals must get their own food.

EXTEND UNDERSTANDING Turn children's attention to the background information on page 8. Ask: How do plants in the story help the animals? How do the animals in the story help the plants? Guide children to see that the fruit and nuts in the story are parts of plants, and that they have seeds that are dropped when the animals eat them.

RESPONSE OPTIONS

SPEAKING Form groups of three children. Have each member choose a character other than Brown from the story. Have each child say what he or she thinks his or her character might say about finding food. The character should talk about why it wants food, what kind of food it wants, how it will find the food, and what it will do with the food.

SCIENCE CONNECTION

TIME FOR Science

Display books and other information about food chains. Have children draw the steps of any food chain that interests them. For example, they might illustrate worm-fish-bear or grass-zebra-lion. Lead children in a discussion of how animals get food from their habitat.

Skill Work

TEACH/REVIEW VOCABULARY

Give each child a set of vocabulary cards. Act out the following sentences as you say them aloud, replacing each vocabulary word by saying *blank:* These are my (eyes). I (pulled) the chair. I am walking (along) the wall. I am (behind) the desk. I am walking (toward) the door. You should (never) be mean. Have children hold up the word that completes each sentence.

TARGET SKILL AND STRATEGY

CHARACTER, SETTING, PLOT Tell children that *characters* are the people or animals in stories, and that characters can be real or make-believe. Ask: Who are the characters in this story? Tell children that as they read a story, they should think about where and when the story happens. Ask: Where does this story happen? Do you think this story happened a long time ago, or could it happen today? Last, tell children that a story's plot is what happens in the beginning, middle, and end of the story. Ask: What was the first thing that happened in the story? What happened next? How did the story end?

STORY STRUCTURE Remind children that each thing that happens in a story leads to the next thing that happens. Together, these things show what the story is about. Tell children that if they keep track of the important things that happen in the story, they will learn more about the characters and where and when the story takes place. They will also be able to tell the plot of the story since they have followed it from beginning to end.

ADDITIONAL SKILL INSTRUCTION

REALISM AND FANTASY Remind children that a realistic story tells about something that could happen in real life. A fantasy is make-believe. Ask: Is *What the Dog Saw* a realistic story or a fantasy? Have children explain their reasoning.

Name _____

Character, Setting, Plot

Read each sentence below.
Then circle the answer that best completes each sentence.

1. The ant in this story is
   a. angry. **b.** lazy. **c.** sleepy.

2. The story happens in the
   a. fall. **b.** winter. **c.** summer.

3. The story takes place in the
   a. front yard. **b.** backyard. **c.** house.

4. The bird gets its food before
   a. Brown does. **b.** the squirrel does. **c.** the ant does.

5. Write three words that describe Brown.

_____

- -

_____

_____

- -

_____

Name _____

Vocabulary

Draw a line to match each word with the word or words that mean the same.

I. along   **a.** things to see with

2. behind   **b.** not at all

3. eyes   **c.** after

4. never   **d.** next to

5. Write a sentence that uses the words *pulled* and *toward*.

_____

_____

_____

Fly Away

SUMMARY This fiction book is about a boy who finds a hurt owl in his yard. The owl is taken to a shelter to get better and then is released back into the wild.

LESSON VOCABULARY

door   loved
should   wood

INTRODUCE THE BOOK

INTRODUCE THE TITLE AND AUTHOR Discuss with children the title and the author of *Fly Away*. Encourage them to describe what they see happening on the front cover. Ask: What type of bird is this? What are the people doing? Why do you think they are waving and where do you think the owl is going? How does this illustration relate to the title, *Fly Away?*

BUILD BACKGROUND Engage children in a discussion of animals and animal shelters. Have them share what they know about animal shelters and what shelters can do for animals. Ask: How do shelters help animals? Have you ever taken an animal to a shelter? Why? Have you ever adopted an animal from a shelter?

PREVIEW/TAKE A PICTURE WALK Have children preview the book by flipping through the pages and looking at the illustrations. Invite them to describe what they see happening on each page and make predictions about the text. Ask: What do you think happened to the owl? What is the boy doing? What is the woman doing with the owl? What do you see happening at the end?

READ THE BOOK

SET PURPOSE Before reading, guide children in setting a purpose for reading the book. Based on your preview of the illustrations, invite children to share what is most interesting to them about the book. Encourage them to share which picture they like best as well as what they would like to know more about. Ask: Why do you want to know more about this illustration? What do you think is happening here? Let's read to find out.

STRATEGY SUPPORT: SUMMARIZE After having children discuss and answer questions about the main idea and events that happen in the book, guide them in *summarizing* the story. Continue to use signal words (first, next, last) to cue the children. Help children identify the key events and main idea in their summary of the story. Ask: What is this story all about? What is the main thing that happens?

COMPREHENSION QUESTIONS

PAGE 3 Where did the boy find the owl? *(in his yard by the wood)*

PAGE 4 Why did the dad call the animal shelter? *(The owl was hurt and a shelter takes care of hurt animals.)*

PAGE 5 Why do you think the woman put the owl in a cage? *(Responses will vary: So it wouldn't get away, so it would stay safe, so she could help it.)*

PAGE 6 What do owls like to eat? *(mice)*

PAGE 8 Why do you think they let the owl go back into the wild? *(The owl was originally from the wild, that's where it lives; it is better for an owl to be in the wild than in a shelter.)*

REVISIT THE BOOK

THINK AND SHARE

1. The boy finds the hurt owl in his yard near a pile of wood.
2. Responses will vary but should show an understanding of the basic events and sequence of the story.
3. Responses should show understanding of word definitions as well as proper usage and context.
4. Responses will vary. Make sure children give reasons for their answers.

EXTEND UNDERSTANDING Explain to children that a *setting* is where a story takes place, and that a story can also have more than one setting. Have children look back through the book to determine the settings in the book *(yard, shelter, forest)*. Have children describe the settings and explain why each is important to the events in the book.

RESPONSE OPTIONS

WRITING Assist the children in writing a short retelling of the story, making sure to include the main events from the book. Use signal words such as *first, next,* and *last* to help children organize their ideas. Then children may illustrate their writing.

SOCIAL STUDIES CONNECTION

Time For
SOCIAL
STUDIES

Talk with children about animal shelters or rescue associations and what they do. Discuss how these organizations help animals and are important to our society. If possible, invite someone from an animal shelter or rescue association to come speak to the class about the work they do. Children may also enjoy participating in a community service activity to benefit the shelter, such as gathering food, blankets, or other necessary items.

Skill Work

TEACH/REVIEW VOCABULARY

Have children practice writing each of the vocabulary words on their own paper. Use each word in a sentence for the children and then help them write their own sentences. You may also wish to say each of the vocabulary words aloud and ask children to determine which two words rhyme with each other (should, wood).

TARGET SKILL AND STRATEGY

SEQUENCE Remind children that all stories have beginning, middle, and an end. As they read, help children keep track of the events in the story by discussing what happens *first*, *next*, and *last*. Be sure to use these signal words to help reinforce the *sequence of events*. Ask: What does the boy do first? *(He finds the owl and takes it to the shelter.)* What happens next? *(The owl gets better.)* What happens last? *(The owl flies away.)*

SUMMARIZE Help children *summarize* the story by asking questions about the main idea. Also encourage them to discuss the events in the story and answer questions about what happens in the book. Ask: What is this story about? What does the boy do to help the owl? How does the owl get better? What happens at the end?

ELL To support greater comprehension, invite children to retell the story in their native languages.

ADDITIONAL SKILL INSTRUCTION

CAUSE AND EFFECT Help children understand *cause* and *effect* relationships by discussing what happened (effect) in the story and why it happened (cause). Ask: What happens at the beginning of the story? *(The boy finds the owl in his yard.)* Why was the owl in the yard? *(It was hurt.)* Continue in the same manner, discussing other events in the story and why they happened.

Name _____

Sequence

Number each sentence from 1 to 4 to put each of the events from the story in the correct order.

_____ A woman from the shelter helps the owl get better.

_____ The dad calls the shelter.

_____ The owl flies away.

_____ The boy finds the hurt owl in his yard.

Illustrate each of the main events from the story.

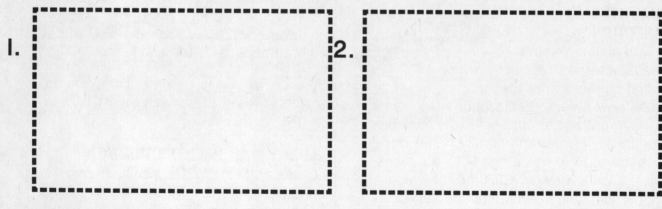

1.

2.

3.

4.

Name _____

Vocabulary

Practice writing each of the vocabulary words twice on the lines below.

door

loved

should

wood

Complete each sentence with the correct vocabulary word.

1. The boy found the owl near some _____ in his yard.

2. Dad opened the _____ when the boy yelled.

3. Dad knew that they _____ call the animal shelter.

4. The boy _____ watching the owl fly away.

What Does a Detective Do?

SUMMARY This nonfiction reader describes what detectives do. It supports the lesson concept that detectives need great ideas and good powers of observation to solve mysteries.

LESSON VOCABULARY

among	another
instead	none

INTRODUCE THE BOOK

INTRODUCE THE TITLE AND AUTHOR Discuss with children the title and the author of *What Does a Detective Do?* Based on the title, ask children what kind of information they think this book will provide. Ask: Have you ever seen police officers asking people questions? Why do you think they were asking questions?

BUILD BACKGROUND Discuss detectives with children. Ask: Have you ever had to solve a mystery before? Maybe you had to find out who in your house ate the last cookie. How did you solve the mystery?

PREVIEW/TAKE A PICTURE WALK Have children look at the illustrations in the book. Ask: What do you think is going to happen in the book? On page 6, ask: what is being held in the boy's hand? Do you know what a magnifying glass is? What does it do? Who uses that kind of tool and why?

ELL Have children look at the illustrations. Point to the blender, toaster, and soap on page 3 and have children provide the English word. Ask: What is wrong with the cookie jar on page 4? Point to the magnifying glass on page 6, and give them the word for the object if they do not know it. Then have children say in English what some of the objects do. For example, "A toaster makes toast." "A blender mixes ingredients." "A magnifying glass makes objects bigger."

READ THE BOOK

SET PURPOSE Have children set a purpose for their reading. Draw their attention to the illustrations. Ask: What do you want to know about the book?

STRATEGY SUPPORT: MONITOR AND FIX UP Remind children that as good readers read, they *monitor* their understanding and *fix up* misunderstandings. Explain that sometimes you have to ask your peers for help. Have children sit in a circle and take turns reading each page. At the end of every page, ask children if they have any questions. Then have the other children answer each child's question.

COMPREHENSION QUESTIONS

PAGE 5 What does a detective do? *(solves mysteries by figuring out what happened)*

PAGE 6 What is a clue? *(It helps tell you what happened.)*

PAGE 6 How do you know that the dog did not break the cookie jar? *(The paw prints are too small.)*

PAGE 7 If you cannot find a clue, what else can you do to solve a mystery? *(You can ask people questions.)*

REVISIT THE BOOK

THINK AND SHARE

1. Possible responses: They both have the same shape. Dogs' paws are bigger than cats' paws.
2. Possible response: I can reread a page if I don't understand something.
3. Possible responses: *cookie, book, took*
4. Possible response: There could be footprints instead of paw prints. The jar probably would have broken from falling on the floor, not by being tipped over.

EXTEND UNDERSTANDING After reading, have children go back and look at the illustrations. Ask, How does each illustration help you understand what is happening in the text?

RESPONSE OPTIONS

WRITING Have children pick out four illustrations. Then have them write one sentence about each illustration using their vocabulary words.

WORD WORK Have children make flash cards with the vocabulary word on one side and the definition on the other. Pair children up and have them quiz each other on the vocabulary.

SCIENCE CONNECTION

TIME FOR Science

Discuss the five senses and which body organs provide each sense. Then have children act out a mystery scene in which the sense is important. Guide their activity by suggesting various events for each sense, for example, hearing a lost cat mewing in a tree or smelling perfume to know who is hiding in the dark.

Skill Work

TEACH/REVIEW VOCABULARY

Review vocabulary words with children. Write the words on the chalkboard, then ask children to pick out the words that have the same sound for the letter o. (*among, another, none*) Have children pick out other words in the reader with the /uh/ sound for the letter o (*someone, sometimes, some*).

TARGET SKILL AND STRATEGY

COMPARE AND CONTRAST Tell children: "*Alike* means telling how things are the same. *Different* means telling how things are not the same." Draw two columns on the chalkboard labeled "Alike" and "Different." Then have children tell how cats and dogs are alike or different. Write their answers in the appropriate column. After reading, have children explain how one of the differences helps solve the mystery. (*A cat is smaller than a dog, so its paws are smaller too.*)

MONITOR AND FIX UP Explain that good readers know that reading has to make sense and are aware when the text no longer makes sense to them. This is *monitoring*. When children do not understand something, they should use *fix-up* strategies to help their understanding. Have children reread text to find answers to their questions. Remind children that if they review what they have read, it will help them understand how things are alike or different.

ADDITIONAL SKILL INSTRUCTION

CAUSE AND EFFECT Use the terms "what happened" and "why it happened" to discuss *cause* and *effect*. Model for children: "'I shared my lunch with my friend, *so* my friend was happy.' What happened is 'my friend was happy.' Why it happened is 'I shared my lunch.'" Ask: What happened on page 3? Why did it happen? Rephrase the answer and write it on the chalkboard: *The jar broke because the cat knocked it over.* Explain that in this sentence *because* is a clue word that points to why something happened.

Name _____

Compare and Contrast

We **compare** objects when they seem alike. We **contrast** objects when they seem different.

1–2. Draw a footprint and a paw print in the box.

3. Write a sentence about how they are different.

_____

- -

_____

_____

- -

_____

Name _____

Vocabulary

Write the word or words that best fit each sentence.

> ## Words to Know
>
> among   another   instead   none

1. The cat sat _____ the cookie crumbs and broken pieces of the jar.

2. Joe wanted to eat _____ cookie.

3. Grandma ate _____ of the cookies.

4. We knew the cat broke the jar _____ of the dog.

5. Use the word *instead* in a sentence.

_____

_____

_____

The Inclined Plane

SUMMARY This selection describes inclined planes as simple machines that make it easier to move objects and people. Pictures and text examine many different kinds of inclined planes, such as ramps, slides, and hills.

LESSON VOCABULARY

against	goes
heavy	kinds
today	

INTRODUCE THE BOOK

INTRODUCE THE TITLE AND AUTHOR Discuss with children the title and author of *The Inclined Plane*. Draw children's attention to the content triangle on the cover. Ask: What other books about science have you read? How do you think this book will relate to science?

BUILD BACKGROUND Remind children that a plane is a flat surface. Then ask them to discuss the various inclined planes they may have used, such as slides on the playground, a hill for winter sledding, or a wheelchair ramp. If possible, show pictures from the Internet or reference books of inclined planes used in the construction of cathedrals and other large buildings or monuments.

PREVIEW/TAKE A PICTURE WALK Have children read the title and spend a few minutes looking at the illustrations and photos. Discuss what these suggest about the selection's content. Look, for example, at the picture on page 8 of the boy lifting the box straight up. Ask: What does his expression tell us about lifting the box? Draw children's attention to the pyramid worker on page 12 and ask: What does this tell us about the history of inclined planes?

READ THE BOOK

SET PURPOSE Guide children to set their own purposes for reading the selection. Children's interest in simple machines or physical activities should guide this purpose. Suggest that children imagine times when they have used simple or complex machines to do something.

STRATEGY SUPPORT: SUMMARIZE As children read, extracting the main ideas for the purpose of summarizing will help them understand and retain what they read. Help young children learn to summarize by suggesting that they retell in their own words as much of the selection as they recall. As an aid, if necessary, draw up a list for children to see of the types of inclined planes mentioned in this selection.

COMPREHENSION QUESTIONS

PAGE 3 Read the second paragraph on page 3. What is the paragraph's most important sentence? *(All that moving is a lot of work!)*

PAGE 5 What are two important details about an inclined plane? *(Possible responses: It's higher on one end and it has a flat surface.)*

PAGE 9 What does the picture tell you about moving things up an inclined plane? *(The boy's expression is happy, so it must be easy to move the box.)*

PAGE 10 How might you use an inclined plane today? *(Responses will vary.)*

REVISIT THE BOOK

THINK AND SHARE

1. Possible response: *All About Inclined Planes*
2. Possible response: Inclined planes are simple machines that make work easier to do.
3. Responses will vary.
4. Possible responses may decribe playground slides, exit ramps, or airport ramps.

EXTEND UNDERSTANDING Go over the photos and pictures in the selection. Ask children to note what the pictures have in common. Guide children to use the pictures in drawing up a description of the essential features of all inclined planes. Ask: What do these pictures tell you that you don't learn from the words?

RESPONSE OPTIONS

VIEWING Bring in or have children bring in examples from books, magazines, or the Internet of many different kinds of inclined planes. Include pictures of inclined planes used in different historical eras, such as ramps used to build medieval fortresses or modern bridges or scaffolding.

SCIENCE CONNECTION

TIME FOR Science

Have children perform a simple experiment by lifting a weight from the floor to shoulder height. Be mindful of safety. Then have children push the same weight up a ramp or slide. Ask them to observe which action required more effort.

Skill Work

TEACH/REVIEW VOCABULARY

Reinforce comprehension by helping children to make a word web around each vocabulary word. Place the vocabulary word at the center of the web. Place all associated words in circles around the main word. Repeat this exercise for each of the vocabulary words.

ELL Distribute clues to the vocabulary words on cards and invite children to identify the word to which each clue refers. Use synonyms, antonyms, phrases, or idioms as clues.

TARGET SKILL AND STRATEGY

MAIN IDEA Tell children that a *main idea* is what an article is all about. The main idea gives the gist of a selection. Guide students in identifying the main idea of *The Inclined Plane* by asking: What do you see on every page of this article? For first graders, a phrase such as *inclined planes* can adequately express the main idea.

SUMMARIZE Explain to children that a summary of an article is a brief statement that gives the main idea and leaves out unimportant details. Invite children to recall the important ideas of the article and restate them in their own words.

ADDITIONAL SKILL INSTRUCTION

CAUSE AND EFFECT Tell children that a *cause* is why something happens, and an *effect* is what happens. Give an example: "Using a ramp to move a box is a cause; the effect is that it is easier to move the box." Focusing on simple machines or physical activities, invite children to think of other cause-and-effect relationships. Point out that sometimes one cause may have more than one effect.

Name _____

Main Idea

A **main idea** is the most important idea about a passage or group of sentences.

Read the sentences below.

> Some people have jobs where they have to move heavy things. Movers move boxes. Builders move things when they build. Drivers move things with their trucks. All that moving is a lot of work!

I. What are the sentences all about? Circle the correct answer.

    a. moving things   **c.** playing with trucks

    b. building things   **d.** having work

Directions Read the sentences below and then fill in the blank line with a title based on the Main Idea.

> You can use an inclined plane to do all kinds of things. You could use it to slide a box up a ramp. You could use it to push a wheelbarrow up a hill. You could also use it to go down a water slide!

2. _____

Name _____

Vocabulary

Directions Pick a word from the box to finish each sentence. Write it on the line.

Words to Know
against   goes   heavy   kinds   today

_____

I. There are many _____ of inclined planes.

_____

2. Inclined planes can help you move _____ things.

_____

3. The girl is pushing _____ the large box.

_____

4. The box _____ easily up the ramp.

_____

5. What types of inclined planes will you use _____ and tomorrow?

123

The Telephone

SUMMARY This book presents information on the invention of the telephone and how it is used today. It supports the lesson concept that the invention of the telephone improved communication in our world.

LESSON VOCABULARY

built	early	learn
science	through	

INTRODUCE THE BOOK

INTRODUCE THE TITLE AND AUTHOR Discuss with children the title and author of *The Telephone*. Also have children look at the picture on the cover. Say: Scientists invent new things. How might this book have something to do with science?

BUILD BACKGROUND Ask children to share what they know about the telephone. Ask: Do you think people had telephones long, long ago? What do you use the telephone for?

PREVIEW/TAKE A PICTURE WALK Have children look at the pictures in the book before reading. Ask: What do you see in every photo? Why are there words below every photo? What is this book about?

READ THE BOOK

SET PURPOSE Have children set a purpose for reading *The Telephone*. Remind children of what they discussed when the title, author, and cover art were introduced. You may need to work with children to have them set their own purpose. Ask: Would you like to learn about using a telephone?

STRATEGY SUPPORT: MONITOR AND FIX UP Remind children that good readers know that what they read must make sense. Tell children that they should check as they read this book to make sure they understand what they are reading. Model by reading the first sentence on page 4. Say: This doesn't make sense. I want to know how old the phones are. Maybe I can find out by reading the caption. Model questions to ask while reading: What does this mean? Does this make sense? Do I understand this? Explain to children that they can use different ways to fix their understanding. One way is to use text features and illustrations. Explain that the photos in this book help you see what the words are about. The captions help you understand the photos. Have children read the text on page 3, then model: Does this make sense? No, I don't know what the first telephone looks like. The picture tells me. The caption tells me more. After children read a page's text, ask: Does this make sense to everyone? Guide children to use the photos and captions to help their understanding.

COMPREHENSION QUESTIONS

PAGE 3 Why did Bell have to learn a lot of science? (*Possible response: Science helps you invent by learning how things work.*)

PAGE 4 Why do you think the author used this picture? (*Possible response: He wanted to show how phones have changed.*)

PAGES 6–7 Is it better for a grown-up to call 9-1-1? Why or why not? (*Possible response: Yes. They can describe a problem better.*)

PAGE 8 Use the picture and caption to help you explain why a school might not be open after a storm. (*It might be too hard or dangerous to travel after a heavy snow.*)

REVISIT THE BOOK

THINK AND SHARE

1. Possible response: He was very smart.
2. 1: Dial 9-1-1; 2: Tell the problem; 3: Stay on the line.
3. Possible response: jaw, law, paw
4. Possible response: It makes it easier to contact people.

EXTEND UNDERSTANDING Point out the simple photo diagram on page 7. Ask: What do the circles tell you? Why is there a finger in the photo?

RESPONSE OPTIONS

WRITING Have children write one or two sentences telling why they liked or did not like this book.

SCIENCE CONNECTION

TIME FOR Science

Display books and other information about 19th-century inventions. Have children choose one invention. Then, ask them to write a sentence about how to use the invention.

Skill Work

TEACH/REVIEW VOCABULARY

Give pairs of children a set of vocabulary word cards. Give them another set with these clues, but first read them aloud: I went to bed before my bedtime. You learn this at school. You do this with a teacher. To enter, you must go ____. This house was ____ by Jack. Have pairs play a memory game by revealing each vocabulary word and its clue.

ELL Use the same cards for this activity. Pair children with more-proficient speakers who will read and act out clues. The non-native English speaker will say and show the correct vocabulary word.

TARGET SKILL AND STRATEGY

DRAW CONCLUSIONS Model: On page 4, I see a picture of early telephones. I know that they don't look like the phones we use today. Based on the picture and what I know about change, I think the phones we use today must do more than the phones of long ago. After children have read page 6, ask: Why do you think the phone number to dial for trouble only has three numbers? *(It is easier to remember.)*

MONITOR AND FIX UP Remind children that good readers know that what they read must make sense. Model questions to ask: What does this mean? Do I understand this? Explain to children that the photos in this book help explain what the words are about, and the captions help you understand the photos.

ADDITIONAL SKILL INSTRUCTION

AUTHOR'S PURPOSE As you preview the book with the children, ask: What do you think the book will be like—funny, sad, serious, exciting? During reading, ask follow-up questions, such as: Were you right about what the book is about? Also ask supporting questions as children analyze the author's purpose, such as: What part of this book seemed serious?

Name _____

Draw Conclusions

Look at the phones on page 4 of *The Telephone*.
Use what you read in the book and what you already know to write the answers for these questions.

1. What is a word that describes what you do to make a phone call?

   _____
   ----
   dial   hang up   _____

2. What do you press to dial a number?

   _____
   ----
   wires   buttons   _____

3. Look at the two phones on the bottom of page 4.
   Is it faster or slower to dial a number with those phones?

   _____
   ----
   faster   slower   _____

4. Look at the two phones on the top of page 4.
   Can you dial a number with those phones?

   _____
   ----
   yes   no   _____

Now, tell more about the conclusion of the book.

5. Write one word to describe how dialing a phone number is different from long ago.

   _____
   ----
   faster   slower   _____

Name _____

Vocabulary

Circle the picture that each word describes.

1. built

2. early

3. learn

4. science

5. through

A Library Comes to Town

SUMMARY A girl and her father in colonial America wish there was a way they could read more books—but books cost money! While working with her brothers in front of her house, Jane overhears a man named Ben Franklin talking about his idea to open a lending library. She runs to tell her father the good news.

LESSON VOCABULARY

answered	brothers
carry	different
poor	

INTRODUCE THE BOOK

INTRODUCE THE TITLE AND AUTHOR Discuss with children the title and the author of *A Library Comes to Town*. Based on the title, ask children to say what they think the book will be about. Have them notice the picture and ask when they think the story happened.

BUILD BACKGROUND Ask children what they know about life in colonial America. Ask: Who is Ben Franklin? When did he live? Where did he live? What is he famous for? What did he do?

PREVIEW/TAKE A PICTURE WALK Invite children to look through the pictures in the selection. Ask them what details the pictures show about life in colonial America.

READ THE BOOK

SET PURPOSE Have children set a purpose for reading *A Library Comes to Town*. Children's interest in colonial America, in Ben Franklin, and in libraries should guide this purpose.

STRATEGY SUPPORT: ASK QUESTIONS Invite children to fill in the L column of their KWL charts after they read the selection. Ask: Were all your questions answered? What else would you still like to know? How could you find the answers to these questions?

COMPREHENSION QUESTIONS

PAGE 3 Why does Jane think her father is unhappy? *(He sighs.)*

PAGE 5 Why can't Jane's father buy books? *(Only rich people can afford to buy books.)*

PAGE 5 What does Jane wish? *(She wishes for a way that everyone could have books to read.)*

PAGE 6 What question might you ask after reading this page? *(Possible response: What did Jane hear that made her happy?)*

PAGE 7 Look at the picture on this page. What is Jane's father using to write with? *(a pen made from a feather)*

PAGE 8 What were some other things that Ben Franklin invented? *(swimming fins, a stove, reading glasses)*

REVISIT THE BOOK

THINK AND SHARE

1. Possible response: how a girl and her father in colonial America find out about a new library coming to town
2. Possible responses: How does it work? Where do the books come from? What happens if you return the books late? How do you get a library card?
3. Unhappy, unfair; Sentences will vary.
4. People borrow books, use the Internet, read newspapers and magazines, listen to storytellers, watch movies, and look at exhibits.

EXTEND UNDERSTANDING Invite children to look at the picture on page 6. Ask them to describe in detail what they see. Ask them what they can learn about life in colonial America from this picture (clothing, hairstyles, houses, cobblestone streets).

RESPONSE OPTIONS

VIEWING Make an exhibit of the children's K-W-L charts. Have the children view their charts and talk about them. Ask children to talk about similarities and differences in the charts. How many children asked the same questions?

SOCIAL STUDIES CONNECTION

Time For
SOCIAL
STUDIES

Children can learn more about Benjamin Franklin by visiting the library or using the Internet. Invite them to research some of his other discoveries and inventions. Children may wish to draw a picture based on the information they find.

Skill Work

TEACH/REVIEW VOCABULARY

Have children find the word *answered* in the selection. Invite them to use the word in a sentence of their own. Continue in a similar fashion with the other vocabulary words.

TARGET SKILL AND STRATEGY

THEME Remind children that *theme* is the "big idea" of a story. Tell children to think about the big idea of this story, as they read. Ask: What do you learn about Jane and her father? Does this story remind you of something that happened in your family? Do you ever visit a library with family members? How does this story relate to you?

ASK QUESTIONS Remind children that to *ask questions* is to ask good questions about important text information. Have children create a KWL chart. K stands for "What I Know," W stands for What I Want to Know," and L stands for "What I Learned." Invite them to fill in the K column after previewing the book. Invite them to fill in the W column, listing questions they hope will be answered in the story. Challenge children to look for the answers to their questions as they read.

ELL Help children to generate questions by modeling some questions for them. Before reading, give them these sentence frames: I wonder if the author will.... I really want to know about....During reading: What does this word mean? What other words in the paragraph can help me figure out this word? What just happened in the story? What is going to happen next? After reading: What did I learn from the story? What do I still want to know? What is this story mostly about?

ADDITIONAL SKILL INSTRUCTION

SEQUENCE Remind children that sequence is what happens first, next, and last. Invite them to think about what happens first, next, and last in the book as they read. They may want to fill in a graphic organizer as they read to keep track of the sequence of events.

Name_____

Theme

Answer the questions on the lines.

1. Why was Jane's father unhappy?

_____
- -
_____

2. What does Jane overhear?

_____
- -
_____

3. What do you think is the "big idea" of this story?

_____
- -
_____
- -
_____

4. When did you have a good idea that helped someone?

_____
- -
_____

5. Draw a picture of how Jane's father looked at the end of the story.

Name_____

Vocabulary

Read the paragraph below. Fill in each blank with the correct vocabulary word.

> **Words to Know**
>
> answered   brothers   carry   different   poor

Jane's father explained that they were too _____

to buy books at the bookstore. "I wish there was a

_____ way to get books," Jane said. "I'm

afraid there is no other way," her father _____.

Later she was working with her _____.

She helped them _____ some chairs onto

the street. She overheard a conversation that made her glad.

She heard that a new lending library was coming to town.

T-Chart

Suggestions You can use this chart to record information in two categories or for various sorting activities. Write the heading at the top of each column.

Three-Column Chart

Suggestions You can use this chart to record information in three categories or for various sorting activities. Write the heading at the top of each column.

Classify

Suggestions Children can use this chart to classify information. For example, pictures of animals could be placed in the circle and then sorted into land animals and water animals in the boxes below.

© Pearson Education

Pictograph

Title _____

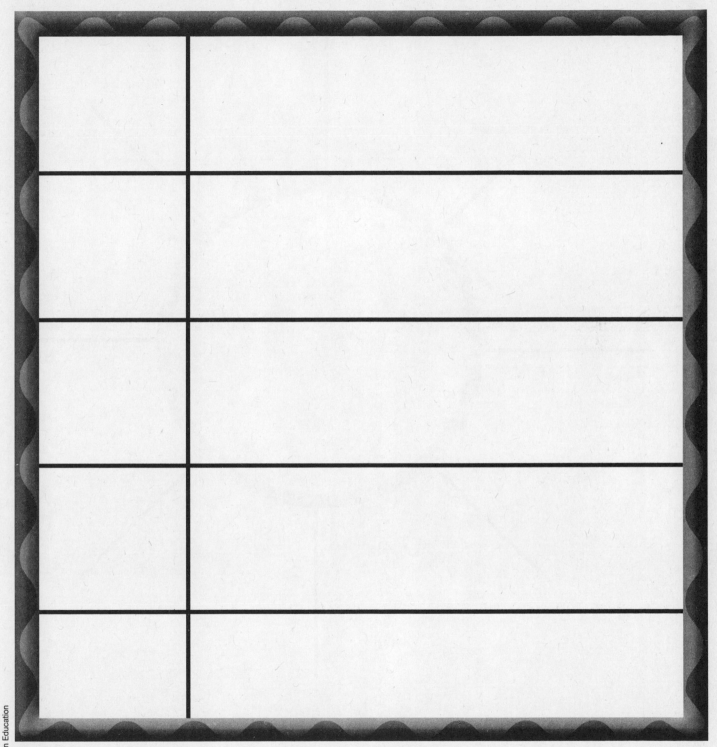

Suggestions Help children make a pictograph to record information. Children draw simple pictures on the chart or on self-stick notes to represent each item. Record the topic at the top of the chart. Some possible topics are: *What did we have for lunch? What pets do we have? What color shoes are we wearing?*

Web A

 Suggestions You can use this chart to activate children's prior knowledge about a topic. Write a major concept in the circle such as *Pets* or *Machines.* Children write or dictate words or ideas that relate to the concept. Write them so that the lines connect them to the circle.

Web B

 Suggestions You can use this chart to activate children's prior knowledge about a topic. Write a major concept in the middle circle, such as *Things at School*. In the smaller circles, children dictate words or ideas that relate to the concept. Additional ideas may be added on spokes coming from the smaller circles.

KWL Chart

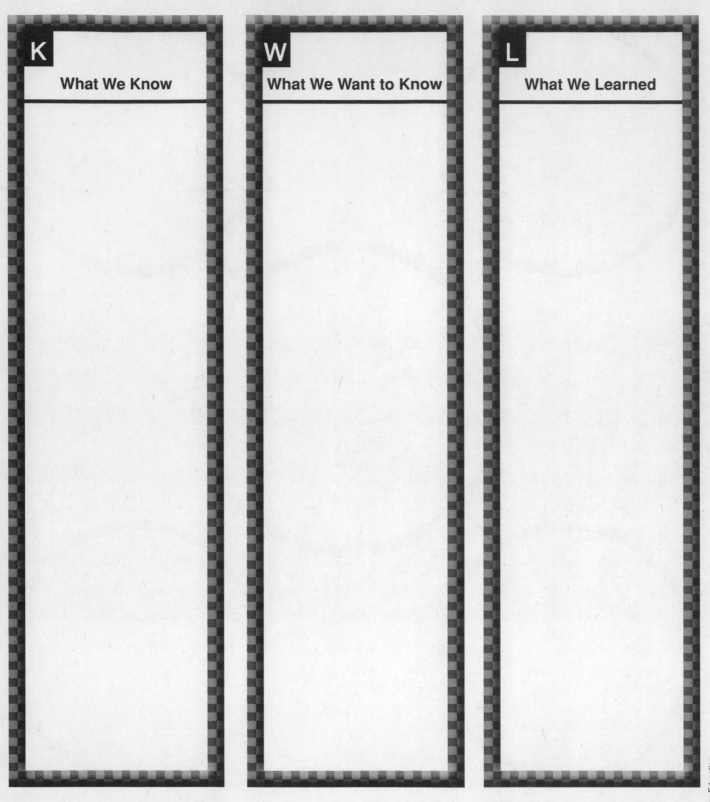

K	W	L
What We Know	**What We Want to Know**	**What We Learned**

Suggestions Have children tell what they know or think they know about the topic. Record their responses in the column **What We Know.** Ask children what they would like to learn. List their questions in **What We Want to Know.** After children learn more about the topic, discuss what they learned. List children's responses in **What We Learned.**

Prediction

Suggestions You can use this chart to help children discuss predictions. Have children suggest what might happen next in a story or other situation. Children may draw a picture and dictate sentences to show the prediction.

Sequence

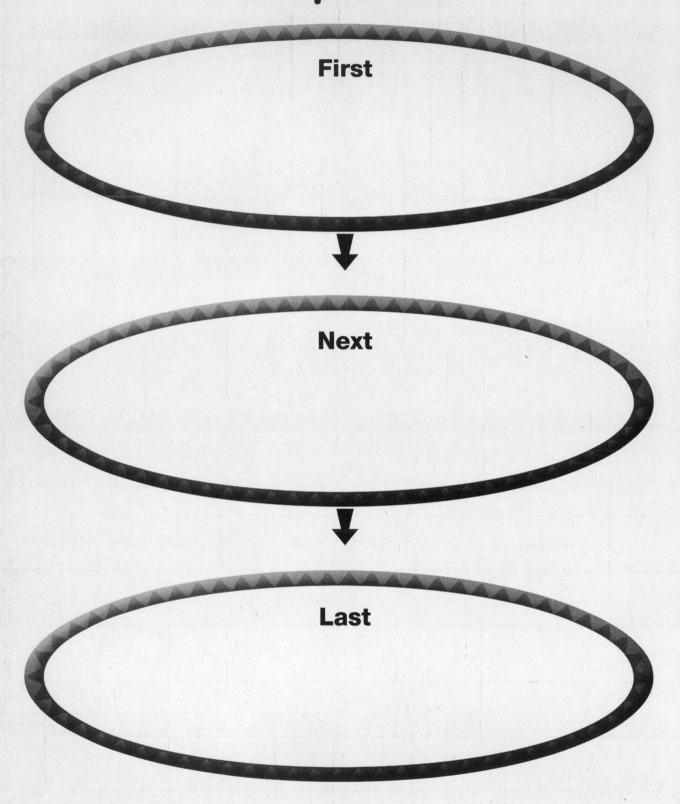

First

Next

Last

 Suggestions Use this chart to help children place events in sequence. Children can draw pictures or dictate what happened first, next, and last.

Story Sequence A

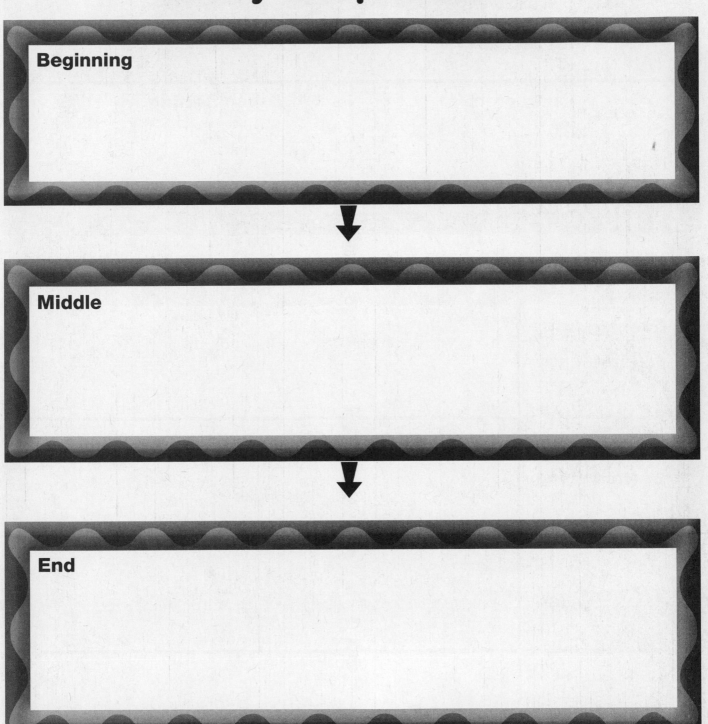

Beginning

Middle

End

Suggestions Use this chart to help children place events in a story in sequence. Children can draw pictures or dictate what happened in the beginning, middle, and end.

Story Sequence B

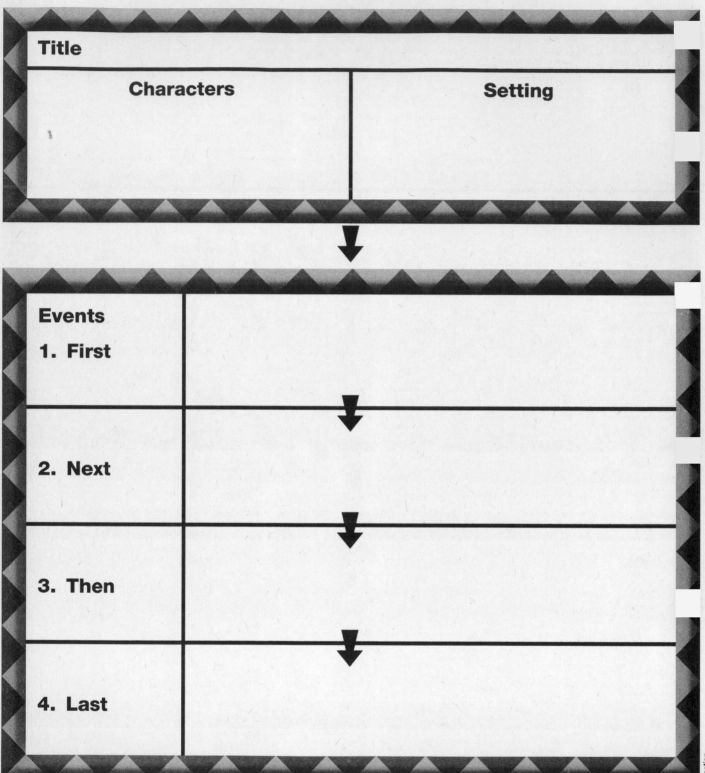

Title	
Characters	**Setting**

Events	
1. First	
2. Next	
3. Then	
4. Last	

Suggestions After recording the title, characters, and setting of a story, children chart the sequence of events. This organizer helps children understand how one event leads to another.

Book Report

Title _____

Author _____

Illustrator _____

Setting _____

Characters _____

Our Favorite Parts _____

Suggestions You can use this chart to record information about a big book or trade book. Discuss where the story takes place, what happens in the book, and how children feel about the book. Invite children to draw pictures of their favorite parts of the book.

Story Comparison

Title A

Characters

Setting

Events

Title B

Characters

Setting

Events

 Suggestions Use this chart to help children compare story elements and structures. This type of activity prepares children for working with Venn diagrams. Children may illustrate or dictate these comparisons.

Question the Author

Title _____

Author _____ Page _____

1. What does the author tell you?	
2. Why do you think the author tells you that?	
3. Does the author say it clearly?	
4. What would make it clearer?	
5. How would you say it instead?	

 Suggestions Use this chart to help children understand the author's purpose and the author's craft. Students analyze what was said, how well it was said, and how it might be said differently.

Main Idea

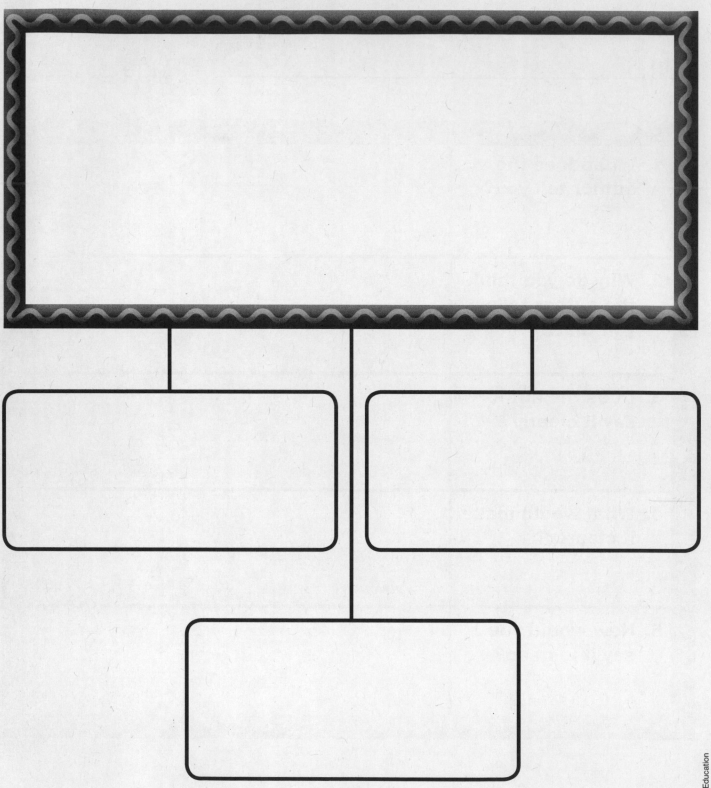

 Suggestions Use this chart to help children understand the main idea of what they read. Ask: *What is the story all about?* Write children's responses in the top box. Have children draw or dictate in the smaller boxes other things they remember from the story.

Venn Diagram

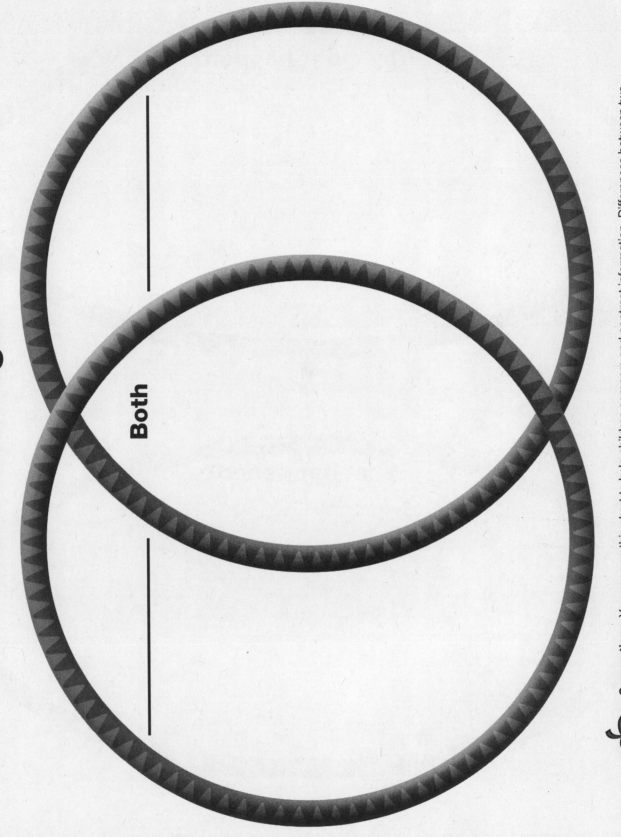

_____

Both

_____

Suggestions You can use this chart to help children compare and contrast information. Differences between two things being compared should be written in the non-intersecting portions. Similarities between two things being compared should be written in the intersection.

Cause and Effect

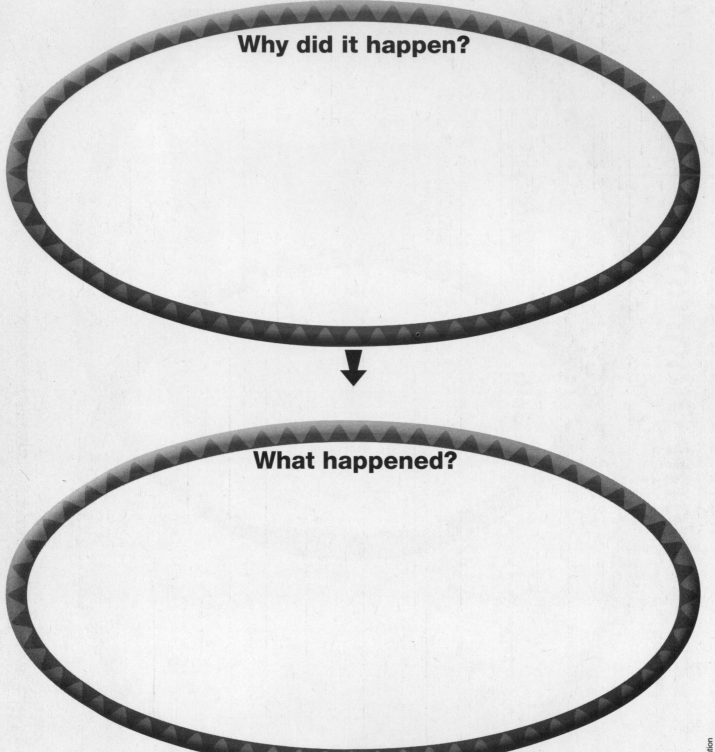

Why did it happen?

What happened?

Suggestions Use this chart to help children understand what happens (effect) and why it happens (cause). Children draw pictures in the appropriate ovals or dictate sentences to show an event. Help children think back and describe or draw what caused that event to happen.

© Pearson Education

Cycle Chart

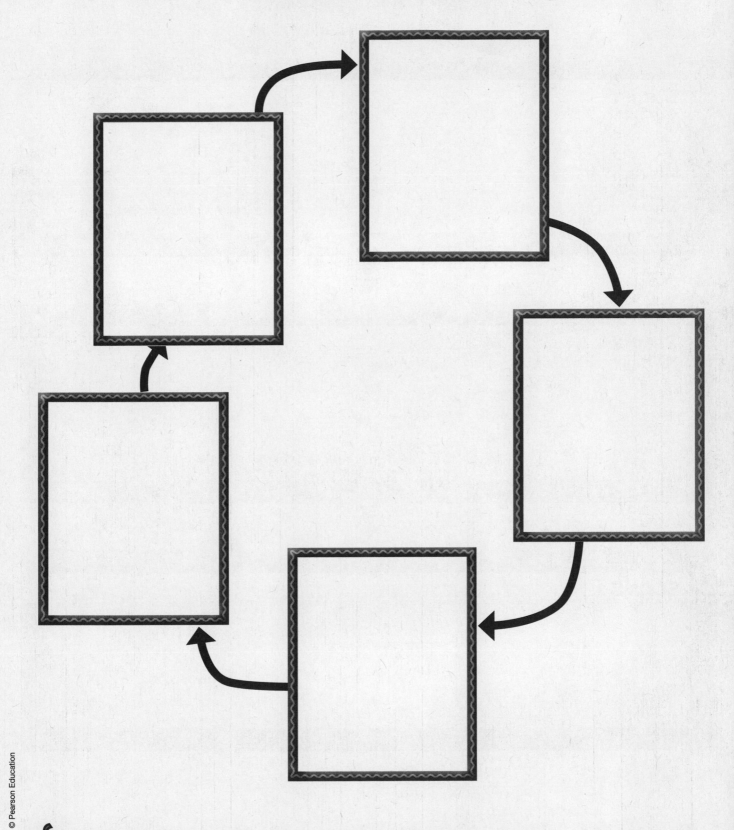

Suggestions Use this chart to help children understand how a series of events produces a series of results again and again. Discuss such questions as: *How does one event lead to another? What is the final outcome?* This chart works well for depicting life cycles.

Steps in a Process

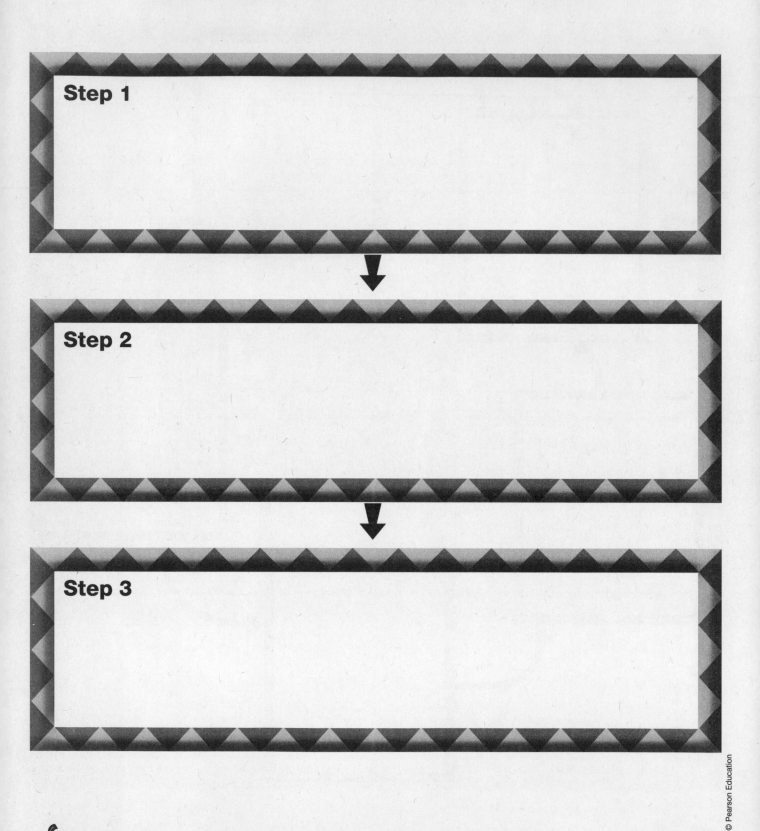

Step 1

Step 2

Step 3

 Suggestions Use this chart to help children break down a process. This chart works well with a how-to activity that has a few simple steps. Students may draw pictures or dictate how to do something.

Writing Topics

Family	Friends	Pets

Hobbies	Favorite Activities

Special Places	Favorite Vacations

Happy Times	Times I Felt Proud

Suggestions Use this chart as a writing resource or interest inventory. Over time, children can generate numerous topics for future compositions.

Letter Format

Dear _____ ,

Suggestions Use this organizer to help children understand the format of a letter. The format can be used for writing to friends, family, or characters from a story.

Numbered List

Title

1.

2.

3.

4.

5.

Suggestions Use this chart to help children list characters, settings, problems, or items that can be found in different contexts or categories.

Answer Key

Leveled Reader Practice Pages

Sam the Duck p. 14

🔊 CHARACTER

Drawings will vary but should reflect story events.

2. Responses will vary. Responses will vary and should reflect an understanding of the character Jack.

Sam the Duck p. 15 Vocabulary

1. on
2. way
3. in
4. drawing should reflect an understanding of the word *on*
5. Drawing should reflect an understanding of the word *in*

Look at Bix p. 18

🔊 REALISM AND FANTASY

Drawings should show a realistic setting or activity.

Drawings should show elements of fantasy.

Look at Bix p. 19 Vocabulary

1. take
2. and
3. up
4. take
5. and
6. up

Rob, Mom, and Socks p. 22

🔊 CHARACTER AND SETTING

Drawings will vary but should depict events from the story.

Drawings will vary but should depict events from the story.

Rob, Mom, and Socks p. 23 Vocabulary

1. help
2. get
3. use
4. wet
5. set

Time to Eat p. 26

🔊 MAIN IDEA

1. c
2. Drawings should depict eating dinner

Time to Eat p. 27 Vocabulary

1. eat
2. her
3. this
4. too

They Help Animals p. 30

🔊 REALISM AND FANTASY

1. a hurt bird
4. a small cat
5. the vet helps animals
6. Possible response given. Dogs can't talk in real life.

They Help Animals p. 31 Vocabulary

1. small
2. saw
3. your
4. tree
5. Children's pictures should be of a hand saw or another type of saw used for cutting.

Animals in the Sun p. 34

🔊 CAUSE AND EFFECT

1. hot
2. fun
3. pond
4. Drawings should show an understanding of the concept.

Animals in the Sun p. 35 Vocabulary

Pictures will vary but should reflect the meanings of the words.

Fun for Families p. 38

🔊 MAIN IDEA

1. b
2. b
3. Picture should reflect understanding of the book.

Fun for Families p. 39 Vocabulary

1. put
2. catch
3. want
4. good

The Play p. 42

↻○ CAUSE AND EFFECT

1. Underlined: Grace and Jake need a job to do; Circled: Grace and Jake will make a horse from old paper.
2. Underlined: We need trees for the stage; Circled: Nate will make trees for the stage.
3. Underlined: The play was funny; Circled: The parents smiled and laughed.
4. Drawings should reflect understanding of cause and effect.

The Play p. 43

1. could	3. horse
2. be	4. old paper

Neighborhood p. 46

↻○ AUTHOR'S PURPOSE

1. park	3. people
2. show	4. share

My Neighborhood p. 47 Vocabulary

1. people	4. Who
2. live	5. out
3. work	

We Look at Dinosaurs p. 50

↻○ SEQUENCE

2   1   3

Drawings should reflect correct sequence of events.

We Look at Dinosaurs p. 51 Vocabulary

1. arrow down
2. three cats
3. boy outside house
4–5. Responses will vary but should reflect understanding of vocabulary.

The Forest p. 54

↻○ AUTHOR'S PURPOSE

1. forest	3. visit
2. show	4. trees

The Forest p. 55 Vocabulary

1. water	4. under
2. find	5. grow
3. food	6. around

Worker Bees p. 58

↻○ COMPARE AND CONTRAST

Possible responses are given.
1. house
2. hive
3. school
4. pollen
5. We both have families.

Worker Bees p. 59 Vocabulary

1. b	4. c
2. a	5. b
3. b	

Nothing Stays the Same p. 62

↻○ COMPARE AND CONTRAST

Pictures will vary.

Nothing Stays the Same p. 63 Vocabulary

1. day	5. always
2. nothing	6. everything
3. become	7. stays
4. things	

Can Hank Sing? p. 66

↻○ PLOT

3   1   2

Pictures should show Hank happy about singing.

Can Hank Sing? p. 67 Vocabulary

1. were	5. sure
2. any	6. every
3. ever	7. own
4. enough	

A Big Move p. 70

↻○ THEME

Possible responses: Sometimes people have to move and leave their friends. They take all their things with them to their new home.

A Big Move p. 71 Vocabulary

very   away   school   friends   our   car   house

The Garden p. 74

↻○ PLOT

1. Drawings will vary.
2. Drawings will vary.
3. Drawings will vary.

The Garden p. 75 Vocabulary
1. X the word *soon*; afraid
2. no X
3. no X
4. X the word *again*; few
5. no X
6. X the word *afraid*; again

Animals Grow and Change p.78
🔄 **DRAW CONCLUSIONS**
A kitten has fur, whiskers, and a tiny cat body.
It will grow larger to become a grown-up cat.
—Some baby animals look like small grown-ups
when they are young.
A caterpillar crawls at first. It becomes a pupa.
It turns into a butterfly.
—Some animals change shape when they grow.

Animals Grow and Change p. 79 Vocabulary
1. know
2. done
3. wait
4. visit
5. push

Seasons Change p. 82
🔄 **SEQUENCE**
1. Spring
2. Summer
3. Fall

Seasons Change p. 83 Vocabulary
does
Oh!
good-bye
won't
right!
Before

A Party for Pedro p. 86
🔄 **DRAW CONCLUSIONS**
1. D
2. E
3. A
4. B
5. C

A Party for Pedro p. 87 Vocabulary
about
enjoy
worry
would
surprise
surprised

Reach for Your Dreams p.90
🔄 **THEME**
People are good at different things. People
like to do different things. People should try to
reach their dreams.

Reach for Your Dreams p.91 Vocabulary
1. great
2. colors
3. over
4. draw
5. show
6. sign
7. drew

Dinosaur Bones p. 94
🔄 **AUTHOR'S PURPOSE**
1. c
2. b
3. b
4. b
5. a

Dinosaur Bones p. 95 Vocabulary
once
mouth
found
took
wild

The Moon Festival p. 98
🔄 **REALISM/FANTASY**
Pictures will vary.

The Moon Festival p. 99 Vocabulary
1. eight
2. moon
3. touch
4. above
5. laugh

A Good Big Brother p. 102
🔄 **CHARACTER, SETTING, PLOT**
Pictures and sentences will vary.

A Good Big Brother p. 103 Vocabulary
picture
remember
room
stood
thought

Does a Babysitter Know What to Do? p. 106
⟳ CAUSE AND EFFECT
1. c
2. d
3. a
4. b
5. e

Does a Babysitter Know What to Do?
p. 107 Vocabulary
1. 2
2. 2
3. 1
4. 2
5. 2
6. 1
7. 1

What the Dog Saw p. 110
⟳ CHARACTER, SETTING, PLOT
1. a
2. c
3. b
4. a
5. Possible response: brown, big, curious

What the Dog Saw p. 111 Vocabulary
1. d
2. c
3. a
4. b
5. Possible response:
   I pulled my wagon toward the park.

Fly Away p. 114
⟳ SEQUENCE
3 2 4 1

Fly Away p. 115 Vocabulary
1. wood
2. door
3. should
4. loved

What Does a Detective Do? p. 118
⟳ COMPARE AND CONTRAST
1–2. Pictures and responses will vary.
3. Sentences will vary.

What Does a Detective Do? p. 119 Vocabulary
1. among
2. another
3. none
4. instead

The Inclined Plane p. 122
⟳ MAIN IDEA
1. a
2. What Is an Inclined Plane?

The Inclined Plane p. 123 Vocabulary
1. kinds
2. heavy
3. against
4. goes
5. today

The Telephone p. 126
⟳ DRAW CONCLUSIONS
1. dial
2. buttons
3. slower
4. no
5. faster

The Telephone p. 127 Vocabulary
1. picture of house
2. picture of sunrise
3. picture of girl at desk
4. picture of scientist in lab coat
5. picture of train through tunnel

A Library Comes to Town p.130
⟳ THEME
1. He is too poor to buy books.
2. Ben Franklin will start a library.
3. Possible response:
   A good idea can help a lot of people.
4. Answers will vary.

A Library Comes to Town p.131 Vocabulary
poor
different
answered
brothers
carry